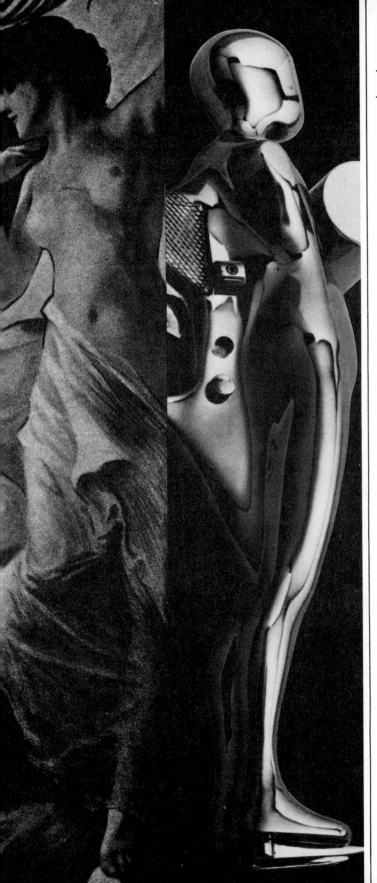

How to See

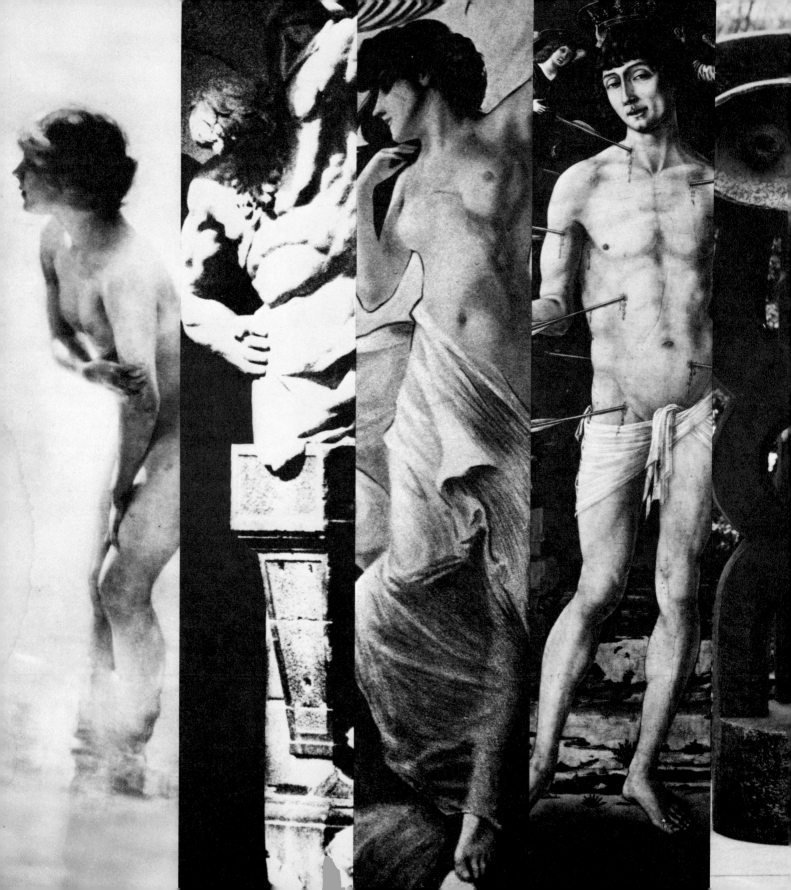

How to See

**A Guide to Reading
Our Manmade Environment**

George Nelson

Little, Brown and Company
Boston   Toronto

for Jacqueline
Mico
Peter

Grateful acknowledgment is made to *Du* magazine for permission to reprint the author's article "About the Design of Sport Equipment" which appeared in the July 1976 issue entitled "Art and Sport."

Library of Congress Catalog Card Number: 77-74658.

C

Published simultaneously in Canada by Little, Brown & Company (Canada) Limited

Printed in the United States of America

Contents

Acknowledgments

All photographs not credited below were taken by the author.

Adidas, 200; Albright-Knox Art Gallery, Buffalo, New York, 83 bottom; Alinari-Scala, 115 top; Ballo & Ballo, Milan, 233; Bayerische Motoren Werke A.G., 97; The Bettmann Archive, 48 right; British Tourist Authority, 110, 111; Brooklyn Public Library, Brooklyn Collection, 128 right; California Department of Transportation, 181; Leo Castelli Gallery, 46; Cavalier Aircraft Corporation, 218 bottom; Centre du Verre de Boussois, 185 right; Nick Chaparos, 138 top; The Coca-Cola Company, 95 top; Downey Museum of Art, Downey, California, 32 bottom left; Du magazine, Zurich, 198, 199; Collection of Charles and Ray Eames, 37; Harold E. Edgerton, MIT, Cambridge, Massachusetts, 83 top; EPA-Documerica, 42 top, 76 bottom, 79 top, 103 bottom; Escher Foundation, Haags Gemeentemuseum, The Hague, 73; French Government Tourist Office, 103–131, 168, 177, 209 bottom; Frigidaire Division, General Motors, 230 right, 231 top right; Gasparini, 123 bottom; Bruno Gecchelin, 140, 166; Peter Gengler, 79 bottom, 82; Collection of Peter Gengler, 36; The Goodyear Tire & Rubber Company, 151 top, 152 left; Greek National Tourist Office, 209 top; George Hall, 207 bottom; Hans Hollein, Vienna, 68–69 top, 70 top; Hans Hollein, Collection of the Museum of Modern Art, New York, 68–69 bottom, 71; ILC Industries, Inc., 190, 191, 192; Italian Government Travel Office, 50; ITT Continental Baking Company, 232; Collection of Carroll Janis, New York, 70 bottom; Courtesy Sidney Janis Gallery, 152 right; Japan Airlines, 183 top; Melvin Jung, 35 bottom right, 80 top; Las Vegas Convention & Visitors Authority, 163; Library of Congress, 29, 33 bottom, 40 bottom left, 40 right, 94 top, 95 bottom, 115 bottom, 148 bottom, 166, 218 top, 223 top; Long Island State Park & Recreation Commission, 180; McDonnell Douglas Corporation, 219 top; The Metropolitan Museum of Art, New York, 21 top, 47, 194, 195, 196, 197; Clichés des Musées Nationaux, Paris, 60; Hans Namuth, 57 bottom left; NASA, 193, 219 bottom; The National Gallery, London, 61; National Gallery of Art, Washington, D.C., 48 left; Jacqueline Nelson, 90, 91 top, 91 bottom left, 211 left; Mico Nelson, 161 bottom; Norwegian Government / Alcan Aluminum, Ltd., 184; Olivetti Corporation of America, 217 bottom; 231 bottom; Pace Gallery, New York, 62, 63; A. Papillon, 185 left; La Photothèque, 187; The Port Authority of New York and New Jersey, 167; Courtesy of RCA Corporation, 94 bottom; Remington Division, Sperry Rand, 217 top; San Francisco Convention & Visitors Bureau, 161 top; Courtesy of the Schwinn Bicycle Company, 213 top; R. H. Shumway Seedsman, Rockford, Illinois, 204 left; Société Bertin & Compagnie, 221; Spanish National Tourist Office, 183 bottom; Ted Streshinsky, 212; Swiss National Tourist Office, 132, 133, 179; Tennessee Valley Authority, 182; Courtesy of Texas Instruments Incorporated, 231 top left; Time-Life Picture Agency, Bill Eppridge, 128 left; USDA Soil Conservation Service, 149; Francisco Vargas, 178; Vermont Development Department, 210 top; Waring Appliances, 230 left; West Air Photography, Weston-super-Mare, England, 176; Westinghouse, 220; West Point Museum Collections, 59 left; Whitney Museum of American Art, 172 bottom.

The author also wishes to thank The Museum of Modern Art in New York for supplying photographs of the following works in their collection: Page 23, Free Form. Jackson Pollock. 1946. Oil on canvas, 19¼ × 14″. The Sidney and Harriet Janis Collection. Page 68 top left, Cadeau (Gift). Man Ray. (C. 1958. Replica after a 1921 original.) Painted iron flatiron with row of thirteen tacks with heads glued to bottom, 6⅛ × 3⅝ × 4½″. James Thrall Soby Fund. Page 78 left, Essex. John Chamberlain. 1960. Automobile body parts and other metal, relief, 9′ × 6′8″ × 43″. Gift of Mr. and Mrs. Robert C. Scull and Purchase. Page 78 right, First Landing Jump. Robert Rauschenberg. 1961. "Combine-painting," 7′ 5⅛″ × 6′ × 8⅞″. Gift of Philip Johnson. Page 80 bottom, Fragment from Homage to New York. Jean Tinguely. 1960. Painted metal, 6′ 8¼″ × 29⅝″ × 7′ 3⅞″. Gift of the artist. Page 142 top left, Target with Four Faces. Jasper Johns. 1955. Encaustic on newspaper over canvas, 26 × 26″, surmounted by four tinted plaster faces in wooden box with hinged front. Gift of Mr. and Mrs. Robert C. Scull. Page 142 bottom right, Proun (Construction). El Lissitzky. Erste Kestnermappe (First Kestner Portfolio). Edited by Eckart von Sydow. 1919–23, Moscow and Berlin. Plate I, color lithograph and collage, 23¾ × 17½″. Purchase Fund. Page 151 bottom, Armchair. Gunnar Aagaard Andersen. 1964. Urethane foam, 30″ high. Gift of the designer. Page 172 top right, The Beautiful Bird Revealing the Unknown to a Pair of Lovers. Joan Miró. 1941. Gouache and oil wash, 18 × 15″. Acquired through the Lillie B. Bliss Bequest.

I have always marveled, in skimming authors' acknowledgments, at the massive battalions assembled to assist in the creation of a book: prides of lofty academics who "criticized the manuscripts and offered invaluable suggestions"; gaggles of tireless researchers who, presumably, researched; loyal secretaries pecking away into the small hours to come up with flawless manuscripts; patient wives without whose unflagging encouragement . . . and so on and on.

Now that this modest opus is in its final stages, I wonder uneasily if I too should have tried something of the sort. But it is too late, and anyway, there aren't that many professors who show much concern about the ways in which we look at our man-made environments.

Still, no man is an island, to coin a phrase, and I too have some debts.

Russell Jalbert, for instance. We knew each other when my office was doing work on graphic design and the planning of field offices for the Social Security Administration. Russell, then Public Information Officer, became interested in the theme and pushed me into doing some exploratory work on visual perception.

Christopher Pullman, now head of Graphic Design for Station WGBH in Boston, was involved in this project, and I remember with pleasure his intelligent and sensitive probing into many aspects of the problem.

But Melvin Jung, a young architectural graduate and a member of our design staff, is the one person without whom this book might never have come to completion. He helped organize the material, wrote innumerable letters asking for illustrations and information, took some of the photographs himself, and went through the work of getting permissions from museums and other sources. A modest estimate of his contribution is that he did the work of at least three people.

I had thought that this ended the acknowledgments, but there is a postscript: on a Friday evening, a week after the above was written, Melvin left the office for his daily bike ride back to Brooklyn. Somewhere along the route he was stopped, stabbed, and left to die. He was "wasted," in the most precise sense of the word, along with a splendid talent and a beautiful selflessness that is the rarest of qualities.

Introduction

A World God Never Made

For an explanation of God's world, the untouched natural environment, there are as many Creation stories as there have been human societies. In the legend with which the Western societies grew up, the whole thing was put together in one good working week, with Man as the ultimate achievement of the Great Designer. Later, we recall, He installed His children in the Garden of Eden, a kind of place environmentalists dream about: a perfect self-recycling environment in which the production of food and consumer goods took place without visible labor, under conditions of zero pollution.

The Garden was His last recorded design, and unfortunately it didn't work. (Is it possible that Omniscience didn't know that Man can stand anything except perfection? Or was the failure planned?) In any event, the serpent appeared, the apple was eaten, all alarms went on, prompt eviction followed, and God disappears from history, at least in His role of designer-creator. There is no record of his involvement in the temple of Solomon, the roads of the Incas, the internal combustion engine, or even the Houston Astrodome. For better or worse, we live in a man-made world, now facing the question of whether it will work any better than the Garden.

The ecosystem, symbolized in the ancient myth, is a mechanism of prodigious dimensions (planetary, no less) and exquisite delicacy. We are just beginning to learn something about it, and with this is coming an awareness that the injunctions in Genesis — "increase . . . multiply . . . dominate . . ." — essential no doubt in their time, have become a sure prescription for catastrophe. There are suddenly quite a few people around who are finding peace, in the business-as-usual sense, just about as scary as war. These fears may well be the first signs of a new level of racial maturity, although a glance at any newspaper makes this hard to believe.

Awareness, when awakened, has a tendency to

spread and expand. It took almost no time at all, once a consciousness of the chemical and thermal pollution of air and water took root, to begin to move on to the idea of *visual* pollution, the introduction of aesthetically offensive elements into the environment. The first targets of this fresh awareness were the obvious eyesores: city dumps, gas stations, signs and billboards, telephone poles and wires.

The crusaders in the battle for environmental beautification called themselves Concerned Citizens and one of their spiritual leaders, briefly, was Lady Bird Johnson, who gave press interviews suggesting that shrubs and flowers be planted around garbage dumps, automobile cemeteries and the like. Here again we were given a demonstration of the blindness afflicting the population, for such recommendations were in the same class as going to Elizabeth Arden for a cancer cure; but at least it got things started. Fixing up deteriorated environments cannot possibly come to anything until the people involved learn to *see* them first, and one of the facts that came through clearly was that visual illiteracy, not billboards and dumps, was the central problem. The physiologists and neurologists got into the act, and presently there were articles appearing which informed us that there was a division of labor in the brain, with a right lobe dedicated to matters visual and a left lobe which concentrated on verbal learning and communication. It was like discovering that an eight-cylinder car was operating on only four, a discovery which made a profound impression on a nation whose pride is based on its putative efficiency. Speculation began: if we could teach children to get both lobes into action, they would start to function better. Maybe there was even money in it. The First Lady's petunias disappeared from the scene, since with us aesthetics is not negotiable currency.

In an effort to find out more about what, and how, people really see, I put together a lecture around a collection of about two hundred color slides and tried it out on a variety of audiences. Einstein has been reported as saying that it is not possible to make an observation unless the observer has a theory to bring to bear on what he is looking at. In a sense, this is as true of laymen as it is of scientists. We all tend to see in terms of what we know, or believe.

The slides used for the test were a seemingly random sequence of images, put together on the basis of associations of shape, use, pattern, color. There was no "story" of any kind. And yet, in four out of five audiences, those asked what they had seen reported that the presentation proved that natural objects were warm, friendly, beautiful, and so on, while the man-made items shown were cold, hostile, inhuman. Another response was that it proved the existence of God, that Man was an exploiter — all kinds of messages that were never put into the show in the first place.

These audiences were made up of managers of corporations, research technicians and scientists, candidates for doctoral degrees, all people whose skills were primarily verbal. The fifth audience was students of architecture and it completely reversed the other responses: the students understood instantly what they were looking at, could see that the transitions from one group of slides to the next were visual, not literary, and by the time the room lights were on again they were making suggestions for improving the presentation. Visual reading, for this group, was as comprehensible as verbal reading. The nonvisual people, on the other hand, found it absolutely necessary to construct a scenario to go with the pictures, just like on TV.

Although the whole project was a strictly amateur effort, since testing audiences is a long way from my professional activities, there was absolutely no doubt that an overwhelming majority of adults, way over 90 percent, cannot see except in the most primitive sense, such as identifying a neighbor's dog or a traffic light. Later on, we will look at some questions, such as why is this the case, but we are not yet through with the matter of visual pollution.

We are not only deficient in seeing (this is true of all advanced industrial societies), but we are also tied to a set of values one might describe as materialistic. The word, as commonly used, tends to suggest a crass, greedy view of life, but in a more precise sense it simply means that we believe reality can be measured, tested, proven in terms of numbers. Galileo was a materialist who tried to prove that the earth was round and that it moved, in a society that had no comprehension of or belief in scientific method; his theories and experimental findings got him into a great deal of trouble with the Church, which was far more impressed by Divine Revelation. We believe in $E = mc^2$ because we have been trained to believe what scientists tell us. When the Bomb went off, this was further, and very convincing, proof that the equation was correct.

The trouble with matters like visual pollution is that *they cannot be measured*, nor can the effects be predicted. If we want to calculate the environmental damage done by, say, car exhausts or factory effluents, we have the people, techniques and instruments needed to come up with precise answers. The dangers to vegetation, animals, fish, and people can be measured and repeatedly tested. But how do we measure the harm done by a superabundance of billboards? How do we even come to a consensus on the ugliness or inappropriateness of such installations? For that matter, how do we define ugliness? There is no Boyle's Law to tell everyone precisely what beauty is. When such matters are put to the vote, what kind of result comes from the polling of opinions on something not really intelligible to the voters?

In the United States, we have a useful special example of the problem in Las Vegas. Here the signs along its main strip are higher, larger, more expensive, and more numerous than anywhere else. The result, when combined with the jukebox glitter of its motels and fun palaces, is a densely packed environment more suggestive of a neon jungle than a normal city. Well, how about Las Vegas? Beautiful or ugly? An expression of uniquely American vitality or social sickness? Would anyone come to see this extraordinary sight if the quick-marriage shops and gaming tables suddenly vanished? What does a Las Vegas tell us, for better or worse, about ourselves? Should it be given a Historic Landmark designation, or bulldozed out of existence? I picked Las Vegas because we have all seen it, on the spot or in photographs, and because there are critics on both sides of the fence.

What it comes down to, all too often, are disputes about "taste," probably the most unreliable of all possible yardsticks. If A finds something beautiful, and B thinks it is not beautiful, but okay, and C is convinced that it is the ugliest thing he has ever encountered, where do we go from there? This is almost always what happens in a society where there is very little experience in seeing. There is always that character who doesn't know anything about art, but knows damn well what he likes. If a public relies on the judgments of a book reviewer, or a film or theater critic, the authority given him seems to be based as much on his *experience* as anything else. One of the things we can build up, in the absence of reliable measuring techniques, is experience. We do this by looking and thinking about what we are looking at.

There is a great deal to see. The world God never made has an astonishing variety of faces, from the carefully tended hillsides of the Philippines to the lush farms and neat forests of France and Germany, to great industrial regions like Ruhr Valley and the slums of Calcutta, Puerto Rico and New York. Their common characteristic is that they are man-made, and in more and more instances they seem to be deteriorating. Our cities have all but pushed out the last vestiges of nature, and the once compact urban centers are disintegrating into unending, featureless sprawl. The freeways and their interchanges are tearing the old cities apart, splitting established neighborhoods, and introducing a new, antihuman scale and tempo.

Such invasions of the urban environment, like the big roads and the monstrous sprawl that goes with them, are not separate elements to be viewed or dealt with on a fragmentary basis, but a unity like the chicken and the egg. What may look like cause and effect is in reality a single phenomenon, an interaction in which it couldn't matter less which comes first. If you start with the roads, then they obviously encourage the sprawl; this further clogs the roads and sets up a demand for more.

The old city, fatally wounded, is left in the hands of its economic dregs, thus accelerating the flight of those who are able to leave — and to pay taxes. Nature continues to recede, bankruptcy approaches, owners and tenants turn to arson, firemen are attacked, the streets become unsafe, the police try to buy more Mace with shrinking budgets, and the yellow-brown smog hangs heavy over everything. The cities begin to move toward clusters of medieval fortresses (getting into a high-rent apartment these days is a little like going through Checkpoint Charlie in Berlin) and the six- to ten-lane roads with their load of vehicles finally merge into a single mobile monster without head or tail. We start to come within view of a nightmarish image of a country flattened by bulldozers, paved solid with asphalt and concrete from sea to shining sea. Thus ends America the Beautiful, not with a bang or a whimper, but to the music of a hundred million cars, punctuated by horns, sirens and the multiple crashes of high-speed pileups. A truly democratic drama in which each of us plays both villain and victim.

Brooding over these now-familiar scenes is the specter of the coming megacities, both dehumanized and dehumanizing, filling the immense "corridors" in which most of us now live, with topless towers everywhere, used indifferently for offices, shops, hotel spaces and dwellings. This new mega-architecture is already with us. With a few exceptions it is generally without scale or relief, and it has no content to which a human being can relate, merely piling cages upon cages like a machine someone forgot to turn off.

This is not another Doomsday lament: last year I visited about twenty U.S. cities, each of which had a shiny new high-rise in the center. What I have been describing is the view one gets from any one of these towers. In the Country of the Blind, when people have tools as powerful as the ones we have built, such scenes of decay and disorder are inevitable.

Visual Literacy

Literacy is the bedrock on which all modern societies rest. Without a very large number of people who can read and write, there is no way to get to the moon or achieve leadership in the pantyhose industry. Any advanced technology, without general literacy, is unthinkable. No bureaucracy, deprived of correspondence, reports on meetings, memoranda, directives, order blanks and invoices, could function. History, under such conditions, would cease to exist, and along with it, the sciences.

When we use the word "literacy" we mean an ability to read, to decode messages in a written language. If we are going to attach "visual" to the idea of literacy, it would seem that we must be talking about an ability to decode nonverbal messages. What is a nonverbal message?

In reality, we deal with such messages more than one might imagine. It is generally believed that a red flag is effective in irritating a bull. By common agreement we go on green lights and stop on red. Driving through an expensive residential district we get silent messages about family income, social status, class tastes, and the like, and if the trip takes us through a slum we get another set of messages, also nonverbal. "Body language" is supposed to be an entire communication system, all silent. Smiles and frowns are the same the world over. Some degree of visual literacy is expected of artists, designers, architects and others who work with forms and colors.

Visual decoding takes place at a great variety of levels, and in this sense it is not basically different from the use of any language. When the Lone Ranger and his faithful Tonto stop at some scuff marks in the desert and conclude that a band of outlaws has passed that way, carrying a ravishing blond captive on a strawberry roan, and that the leader's horse had recently thrown a shoe, we marvel at their skill in getting so much information out of some disturbed earth. What these two would do if confronted by Picasso's *Guernica* is another question. Reading a painting takes another set of skills

Again, we can connect with the written language: an ability to follow the instructions for adjusting a carburetor does not necessarily guarantee that the same skill would take its owner through *Ulysses*. Furthermore, there are many written languages, and to learn any of them takes time and effort.

The classic reader of visual clues in English is, without any question at all, the one and only Sherlock Holmes. He can look at a watch belonging to Dr. Watson and, in a flash, relate the sad history of the downfall of the good doctor's alcoholic brother. He can glance at a stranger hesitating at the entrance to their flat on Baker Street and decide that this is a doctor, just out of military service, recently wounded in Afghanistan. Watson, in his role of the perfect stooge, is always astounded by these visual

readings, which always have to be explained by the Master.

Nonverbal reading is mysterious for more people than Dr. Watson, for it is baffling to find someone with eyes no better than our own, who sees things we are unable to perceive. In the course of following occupations which make few demands on any but verbal skills, we do very little real seeing of any kind. All this is one face of the visual coin, so to speak. The other has to do with the kind of information we bring to the act of seeing.

Holmes will look at a cigarette ash at the scene of a crime and know the brand, not merely that it is an ash. In other words, his seeing is coupled with a great deal of specialized knowledge: he is a student of chemistry, an expert in poisons, he has files of criminal cases, he reads all the papers, he knows which stolen gems belong to whom. When he "sees" in ways impossible for Dr. Watson, he is seeing with the aid of an enormous memory bank of accessible information. We all see with what we know, although few of us are in the class of Conan Doyle's immortal creation.

It is a general rule that we like what is familiar to us and that we tend to back off from anything unfamiliar. Company managements are acutely aware of this, and one of the results is that products on the market at any given moment tend to look alike, whether they are cars, household furniture or stereo receiving sets. Furthermore, the lower the level of education, the stronger the tendency to recoil from the new and unfamiliar. The reason for this is simply that the educated person is more familiar with more things, and hence more flexible in his responses. For the same reason, the more "mass" the market, the more conservative the product.

In visual reading, like verbal reading, the completeness of the reading relates directly to the quality of the reader's stored information. An FM broadcasting station produces an absolutely uniform transmission of information. If the broadcast is picked up in one case by a pocket transistor and in another by a high-fidelity system, there is obviously a tremendous difference in the quality of the message as received.

Still another way of saying all this is to describe seeing as a *transaction* between transmitter (the sight) and receiver (the viewer). A cat may look at a king, as the old saying goes, but the visual message is more interesting if the onlooker also knows what a king is. Visual communication, therefore, is not unlike other kinds of communication in that it is broadcast and received and in that it uses a code or language which has to be intelligible to the receiver.

This becomes instantly apparent when we turn to modern painting. In the art of the nineteenth century and earlier, a painting was invariably *a picture of something*. You could look at it and see that the subject was a dog or a family group, a still life, a landscape. At the popular level of viewing, identifying the subject and perhaps the sentiment was sufficient. In this sense traditional painting is not unlike what we get on a TV screen: a story illustrated by photographic images. If the police are chasing the villain, we see cars screaming around curves, going off cliffs; gunplay; and the inevitable finale.

Specialists on traditional representational painting take the act of seeing well beyond identification of subject matter. They know about painting techniques in use, they know why such pictures were made rather than others, they are familiar with the artists' patrons and clients, they know something about the social context, and they have a great deal of general information which helps them to compare the quality of one artist's work with that of another. Most of this kind of thing is inaccessible to the average museum goer, which is why more than one museum director will describe the majority of visitors as visually illiterate. They simply have no

vocabulary of value, and very probably no idea that nonverbal languages exist.

It is when subject matter, perspective and other familiar elements in painting disappear, as in modern painting, that the absence of nonverbal comprehension comes out into the open. Why does a museum show a cluster of four aluminum boxes as art? What gives value of any kind to a painting which is nothing more than a white or black surface? Léger's people look like boilers: where has he seen such people? Why do the Cubists chop up guitars, tables, newspapers and bottles and put them back together all wrong? The usual responses, going back at least sixty years to the New York Armory Show, are that the artists are crazy; it is fairly standard for people to react to newness with nervous hostility. It is also possible, however, that the artists are sane and that the world they are painting is crazy.

Way back in 1959 at the U.S. National Exhibition in Moscow, which my office had had the good luck to design, there was a large show of American artists, very carefully selected by Edith Halpern to illustrate the full range of contemporary styles and trends in U.S. art. The Russians, long limited to an official style not unlike that of the old *Saturday Evening Post* covers, jammed the gallery every day.

One afternoon a Soviet visitor, a man in his middle years, began asking questions of one of the guides about some of the more far-out examples. The guide, a young American student, selected for her ability to speak Russian rather than for her knowledge of art, had trouble explaining what this or that picture meant and why the artist had painted it as he had. The visitor got impatient, then angry, and began shouting, "I demand an explanation of this rubbish! I am a Soviet citizen, I have a ticket to the exhibition, and I have a right to know!" The rattled girl sent for help, but the noises got angrier and it began to look as if a small riot were in the making. We were saved by another visitor, who tapped the enraged Soviet citizen on the shoulder and said, "Comrade! Shut up. You are making us all look like fools."

The shouting stopped abruptly. Our savior continued in a calm voice, but loud enough to carry through the room, "Comrade, the problem is not with these paintings, but with you. Through some misfortune in your upbringing, you are under the impression that a painting is a kind of window. You look through it and see a scene, like a bowl of apples or a battle or a portrait. But that isn't what a painting is at all. It is some pigment on a flat surface; maybe it shows something you can recognize, but it is also possible that all it shows you are shapes and lines and colors."

There was not a sound in the crowded room, and the stranger continued. "Imagine, my friend, that this is not a painting gallery, but a display of important mathematical equations. Would you then start shouting at this nice young woman and get her upset by demanding that she explain these to you? Of course you wouldn't. You would realize that you don't understand mathematics, and keep quiet. Here we have paintings, and you don't understand them either. Why don't you just look at them without disturbing everyone and then, when you go home, perhaps you could find some books that might help you begin to learn something about art. Try to remember that the rest of us here are also Soviet citizens and that your uncultured behavior is giving our American guests a very bad impression."

He drifted off into the silent room, carefully looked at each picture, and presently vanished. The moral, I suppose, is that the U.S.S.R. has its full share of visual illiterates too, but his point could not have been made with greater force or clarity: a painting is not a picture window; it is a painting.

To see, as Dr. Joshua Taylor of the National Gallery has observed, is to think. To think is to put together random bits of private experience in an orderly fashion. Seeing is not a unique God-given talent, but a discipline. It can be learned.

This morning, in a shop dealing in instruments and equipment for musicians, I watched three young men deciding whether or not to buy a drum. They clearly had a fund of accumulated experience with drums, and they were busy testing it for sound, examining its construction and hardware, and stroking its surfaces to judge the quality of its finish. There was none of the "I don't know anything about drums, but I know what I like" kind of thing. They *knew*, and it was exciting to watch the senses of hearing, sight and touch working in combination with their experience.

The questions that come up when visual matters are being discussed with almost any group except designers or artists almost invariably have to do with the possible value of being able to see. Does the visual literate have better taste than other people? Why should I learn how to "read" buildings and steam irons? Will I understand art better? Do you mean that seeing is always a kind of detective work? Where do beauty and ugliness come in? Why do you talk about experience and performance and always ignore the aesthetic element? Can it help my career? How?

It is very revealing that our entire social conditioning pressures us into looking for the exchange values of anything we acquire, whether property or knowledge. Never has anyone asked me if seeing makes life richer, or more entertaining. It has to be *worth* something.

This is not the place to discuss the value of our values, but we might note in passing that if an ability to read words helps us get around, make a living, and add interest to our lives, so does seeing. *Why* one decides to learn anything stems from a broad range of motivations, and if one of them is a desire to help improve our physical environment, this is as good as any other.

I'd like to get on to the question of *what* we see. For most of us, there is precious little nature and an enormous assortment of man-made things. The single common element in all man-made things is that they are *designed*. One might say that this holds for nature as well: a leaf, a ladybug, a lizard can all be described as delicate and infinitely complex designs. But I think that if we stick with what we are most familiar with, the man-made world, we will have all we can handle. It is also less complex.

The reason for bringing in the idea of design is that you can't build or make anything without it. A child making a sand castle has some kind of picture in his head that is telling him what to do next. The designer of the first bow and arrow had somehow stumbled on the idea (through observation) that a bent piece of wood with a string in tension attached to both ends will propel an arrow. And so it turns out that if we really want to see the physical environment within which we spend most of our time, we do have to understand something about design and the design process. In other words, seeing and design are related, just as seeing and thinking, seeing and feeling are related.

Everyone makes design judgments through seeing. Why do more people buy metal station wagons with fake wood pasted on their sides than the simple painted metal models? Why do people buy "Mediterranean" kitchens, although there is nothing especially Mediterranean about sinks or refrigerators? Why are more "Colonial" clocks (with electric batteries) sold than "modern" clocks (also with electric batteries)? Who decides that a sophisticated piece of electronic equipment, such as a TV set, has to go into a "French Provincial" cabinet? Whatever we think of these judgments, they are nonetheless design decisions and people make them all the time.

Since most cars appear to run much like other cars, decisions to buy are made, not on mechanical

quality, but on their appearance. These days vinyl roofs and "opera" windows seem highly acceptable. What does an opera window mean to a prosperous plumber who would have to fly eleven hundred miles to see an opera? How much of the basis of such decisions has to do with social emulation rather than an evaluation of design quality?

The same goes for art. In a functionally blind society, the role of art is widely misunderstood. Art, for the visually illiterate, has some vague connection with "beauty," the "finer things," "aesthetics," and none at all with its real role of coming to grips with various aspects of perceived reality. In this sense, art is not that different from science, which is also involved in discovering ways of understanding reality. The difference lies not so much in the aims as in the method. Science insists on precise measurements and searches for laws which explain phenomena. Art tends to rely on an intuitive, visual approach. Even these distinctions are not absolute: many great scientists and mathematicians have worked intuitively; many artists show a strong intellectual approach in their work.

In all cases, whether we read the findings of scientists or of artists, *we have to read*, which means we have to know the language. The language of vision uses light, shape, color, texture, lines, patterns, similarities, contrasts, movement.

One example of this, illustrated later on, is the case of the crushed can. A soft-drink can of aluminum, say, drops into the street and is run over by a truck. It is still an aluminum can, but it is no longer a smooth cylinder. A moment ago it had a value, with its contents, of perhaps thirty-five cents; now it can be sold as scrap to a recycling center for a half cent. Applying a different theory of value, however, we can say that through the intervention of the truck, a bland cylinder has been transformed into a sculptural object of unexpected richness, and its value is no longer monetary but visual and tactile.

Seeing, then, is also dependent on the value system of the observer.

A long-delayed question (I really should have brought it up much earlier) is, how does it happen that very young children, all of whom quite naturally absorb great quantities of visual information, grow up to be visually illiterate? The answer, as far as I can make out, is that this early capability is simply beaten out of them by the educational process.

Modern societies are all very conscious of the importance of education and spend enormous sums on school plants and administrative systems. So we cannot blame visual illiteracy on a lack of education. We have to consider the kind of education.

Americans, during most of our history, have tended to assume that education is "good" and that more of it is better than less. Where money could have any effect, we have always supported education generously. The first free public high school was opened in 1821, Webster's dictionary appeared seven years later, the land-grant colleges began in 1862. The widespread approval of verbal education reached a kind of peak in Andrew Carnegie's gift of nearly three thousand public libraries. Looking more closely at these impressive achievements, what we see are words and numbers, numbers and words. This is what education was all about and until recently no one thought to criticize or complain.

Why the emphasis on words and numbers? The answer is that this is what an industrial society needs, and with this answer we suddenly see that education is not a fixed good, applicable to all times and places, but a process perceived differently, depending on dominant social needs and beliefs. Technology needs people who can read and write, add and subtract.

There would be no questioning or criticism of education if the society were not now transforming itself in a very massive way. We are not quite clear about what it is turning into, but there is no doubt at all that something big is going on. Just one little straw in the wind is the steady, persistent decline of verbal literacy in the population as a whole. The high schools are turning out graduates who do not seem to be able to read or write anymore. There is a theory that TV is the cause of this, that people are taking in more visual information than they used to, and hence tending to put less importance on words. Perhaps this is so, but for me TV is not a visual medium, basically, but a technique of telling very simple, even primitive, kinds of stories which are then illustrated by moving pictures. Verbal skills, in this process, are being downgraded below the level of books or radio, but the corresponding upgrading of visual skills is questionable.

A more believable explanation, in my view, lies in the accelerating tendency of a technological society to turn its people into things. In almost any industrial process, people represent the one element that is not predictable and totally controllable. People come to work late, goof off, make mistakes, sabotage, don't think about what they are doing, get sick. A human individual, compared on this basis with, say, a ball bearing, is a bundle of headaches for plant managements. Everything possible is being done to get people out of the process, through automated machines, quality-control devices and computers, and one reads predictions that the factory population will eventually decline to 5 percent of the total population. Until that happy moment, every pressure imaginable is being used to make people more dependable or, to put it differently, to convert them into something that can be processed uniformly, like inorganic materials.

At the consumer end of the scale something similar goes on with the pressures of advertising and the dehumanization of shopping. A consumer, at least from the technocrat's point of view, is a programmed mechanism (still with some organic defects, alas) which buys on command those items needed to keep industry going at a satisfactory rate.

These pressures are entirely understandable, given the specialized aims of a technological society, which have little or nothing to do with the improvement of the human condition. They have not been entirely unsuccessful, either. Modern populations tend to be joyless and unmotivated; work has lost its original meanings, which had to do with its role in fostering personal growth; play, which is the other side of the coin, has become more and more automated and meaningless; and cities, which people are supposed to build for people to live in, are being abandoned wherever there is money to pay for the getaway. Why indeed should such masses of crippled humanity continue to maintain an interest in verbal literacy, or anything at all aside from the available forms of escapism?

If the pressures and their partial success are understandable, so is the resistance to them, for people simply are not designed for easy conversion into zombies or ball bearings. The first wave of rebellion on a large scale was the counterculture of the sixties, and while this has seemingly subsided for the time being, there will be others if for no other reason than the fact that the technocratic establishment is tripping over its own feet more and more frequently. The global transformation now going on can be identified easily enough by simply keeping count of the mounting series of crises of all types, whether inflation or recession or unemployment; the breakdowns of political systems, law and order, the nuclear family; or the impotence of top leadership.

One idea worth consideration is that what is going on in this vast transformation is a shift from materialist values to others based on the physical and emotional needs of live human beings. If so, this would not be the first time the pendulum has swung back in this fashion. What would follow, then, would put the right lobe of the brain back in business, and sensory development would take a high priority in a radically modified educational system.

Road Map

Both books and road maps take us places, but there is a basic difference between them. Books, as a rule, are *linear*, which is to say that the writer has some idea of a theme which he develops from a beginning into a middle and on to an end. You have to move along the line set forth or run the risk of missing something important. Whodunit fans consider it unsporting to peek at the final pages when the reader is only partway into the story. The perfect example of linearity is an instruction manual about how to put a kit together: leaving out a step always makes for trouble and it could prove disastrous, as when an assembly is soldered together so that the part overlooked cannot be inserted.

Road maps differ from such books in that they show *networks*, and it doesn't matter in the least to the mapmaker where you start and end up. A map works for the user because he knows where he is and presumably has some idea of where he plans to go. All the map does is show paths between starting point and destination.

This book is very much like a road map. It starts with the fact that the number of things to look at approaches infinity. It assumes that the reader has an interest in sharpening his visual skills, and, as in the case of the map, it does not matter where he starts, for the process of extracting information from nonverbal material is always pretty much the same.

While the book was given its title *How to See* because it seemed like a reasonable description of what it is about, a more accurate title would be *How I See*. Seeing is an intensely personal matter; no one else can do it for us. What is even more to the point is the fact that we see in the light of accumulated experiences, stored information, private interests and entrenched beliefs. The interest of any theme does not lie in any hierarchy of subjects, but inside the reader and his ability to decode the messages. I once bought a book dealing with poetry and mathematics on the strong recommendation of a friend, and got nowhere with it. Clearly my decoding machinery, in this special instance, was inadequate. We have all had such experiences, whether with books or things looked at. A lady from Nebraska whose acquaintance I made on a plane had just finished a concentrated course in hairdressing in Paris, and told me with a sigh of relief that she was finally out of that miserable city and would never have to see it again. Others exposed to Paris see it differently.

So we come, as always, to the question of Truth. What is it? Is it still living at the bottom of a well? How do you measure it? Who is the final arbiter? All such questions have been asked over and over again for a very long time, and it seems unlikely that the situation is going to change in the near future.

What we are left with is the reality of our varying abilities to use our eyes. What this takes us to is not any particular brand of truth, but rather the possibility of uncovering many *levels of meaning*, and this is dealt with repeatedly in the pages which still lie ahead. Seeing, which cannot be disconnected except in the most mechanical sense from the overall workings of the brain, relates to the traditions in which we have been raised — ideas imbedded in childhood, the millions of bits of random information stored in our private memory banks, either conscious or subconscious — to the rigidity or flexibility with which we respond to the unfamiliar or, better still, to the familiar suddenly seen with fresh eyes. The seeing is always conditioned, but at the same time it is uniquely personal and private.

As I look at familiar urban and roadside environments, what I have gradually come to see is a national scene of prodigious ugliness and disorder, utterly disrupting in its effects on the natural world and equally brutalizing for the populations exposed to it. My perceptions of contemporary reality conform with this personal bias, and the written comments throughout the book naturally reflect it. This is what I mean by "uniquely personal and private" seeing. It is also true that since no one is unique in every sense, there are inevitably those who will agree with my perceptions. But even this support is no guarantee of "truth."

I think that the most we can do, given the impossibility of finding a basis of quantifying responses which are conditioned, intuitive and not subject to measurement of any known kind, is to come to a relaxed agreement that, just as there are "sermons in stones and books in running brooks," to take Shakespeare's view, there are indeed messages being transmitted by inanimate objects which can be "read" by anyone capable of seeing what he is looking at. I believe that we might also agree that these messages come in terms of levels of meaning which are different, ordinarily, for different observers. For our purposes, that is good enough.

While there are exceptions here and there, you will find that most of the material in this book deals with urban scenes and fragments thereof, if for no other reason than the fact that this is where the overwhelming majority of us spend our time. Most of the books on seeing I have run across either have a physiological or neurological base, or deal with art in some form or another. I have omitted the first because I think that for a beginning foray into the area they are not especially relevant. Books on understanding art exist in fair supply. Parenthetically, for whatever it may be worth, my view of the work of many contemporary artists is that at first glance much of it appears to be crazy, but that further examination and thought strongly suggest that it is the society which has abandoned sanity. The artist, in continuing to pursue his traditional role of sensitive observer and reporter, is merely pointing this out.

Communications

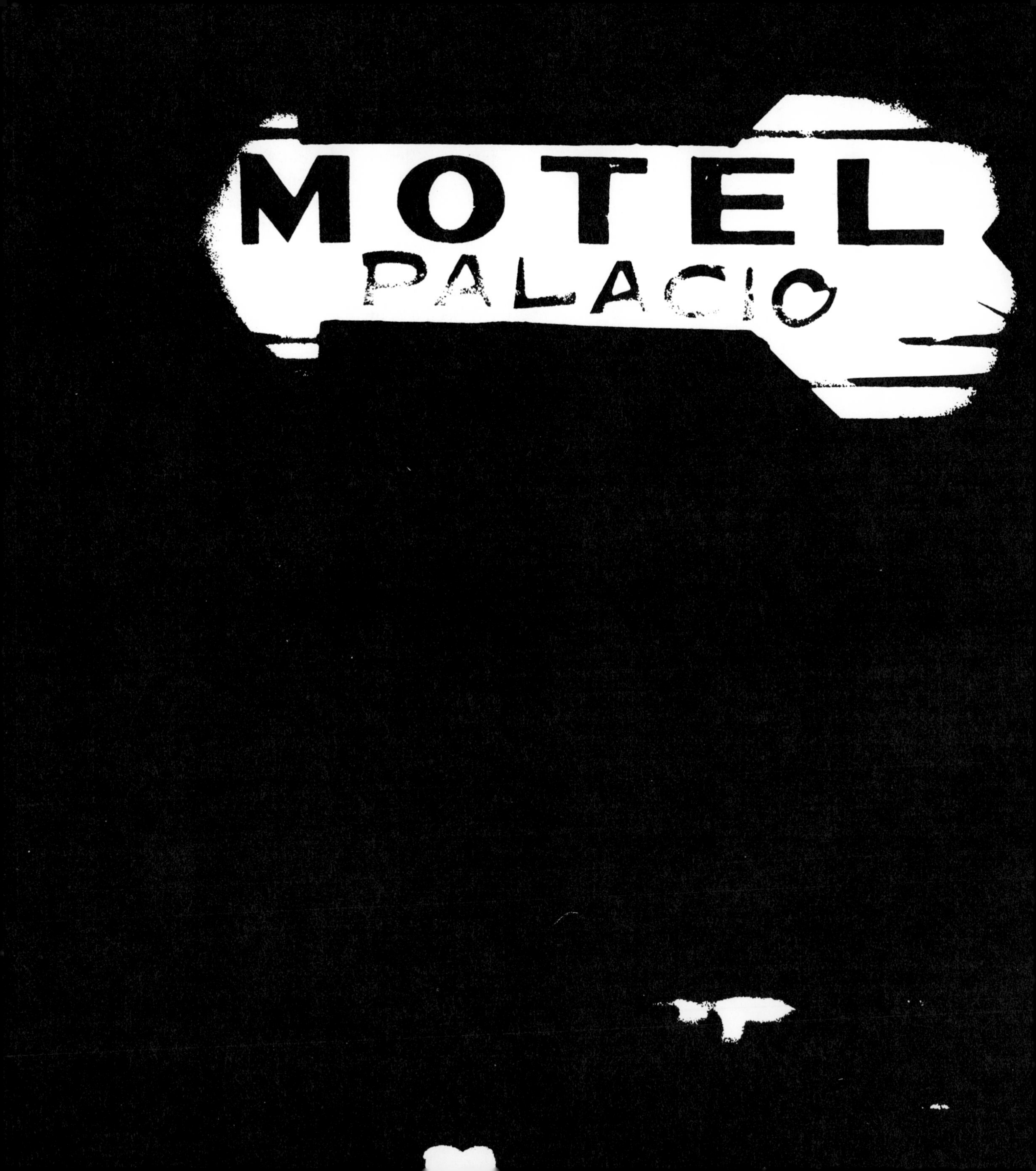
MOTEL
PALACIO

Letterforms

To be able to read we have to learn the letters of the alphabet. The word "literacy" has a Latin root that means "letter." An old English word for "illiterate," hardly used anymore, is "unlettered."

All around the world, in a hundred countries, classrooms resound with the piping voices of small children chanting their ABC's.

After the letters come words, phrases, sentences, and a lot of rules of grammar.

Seeing is involved in learning the alphabet, naturally, and children can presently identify any letter in a wide variety of shapes and sizes. Then the seeing stops.

We are going on, very briefly, to the next lesson, the one the schools neglect to teach. It has to do with the form of the letter itself. The letters in any alphabet belong to a "family" of forms in which the shape and style of any letter is similar to that of all the others. We understand this in a general way: we would not use the same family of letters for a circus poster and a wedding invitation, for traditions have

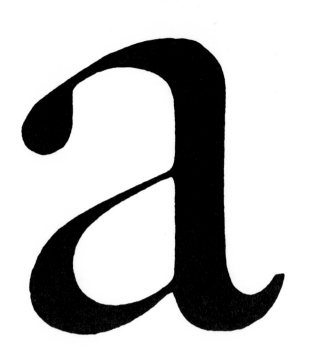

grown up which tell us that a typeface appropriate for one use is not right for another.

Letterforms can be graceful, clumsy, brash, vulgar, elegant, modern, old-fashioned, dense, delicate. Then there is the matter of legibility. If any of us had to pick the type for a telephone book, where as much information as possible has to be packed into the smallest space, we would examine all kinds of type styles, reduce them to the limits of legibility, and then begin to make judgments about which works best.

The formal meaning of letters, which has to do with their form or style, is not so easy to put into words. There are professionals, typographic designers, who develop great skill in identifying the styles of the different families of letters, and in selecting the best ones for specific uses. ''Best,'' by the way, means what the designer thinks is best; there are no systems for accurate qualitative measurement.

Sunday Gazette

As an example of such problems, we have the name of an imaginary newspaper. How do we decide which type style is "best"? In making a choice we find we are reaching back into our memories of other newspaper titles and we also try to think of the character of the paper and to match this with a suitable family of letters.

You have already noticed that one of the lines is incomplete. To fill in the missing "S" a type designer would take his clues from the other letters, and he could probably do a fair job of reconstruction without other help. You might try it. The exercise will demonstrate either that re-creating the letter is not as easy as it looks, or that you picked the wrong profession and should have become a designer.

S S S S S   **Sunday Gazette**

S S S S S   **Sunday Gazette**

S S S S S   Sunday Gazette

S S S S S   **unday Gazette**

S S S S S   Sunday Gazette

Numbers (1)

Numerals, like letterforms, have changed over the centuries. The biggest change in the West was the shift from Roman to Arabic numerals. If anyone wonders why, try multiplying MDCCXXXVII by CXXVIII.

Now, with electronic scanners, machines can also read numbers. The top line has "people" numbers, the second can be read by people and magnetic scanners, and the last is legible only to machines.

0123456789

0123456789

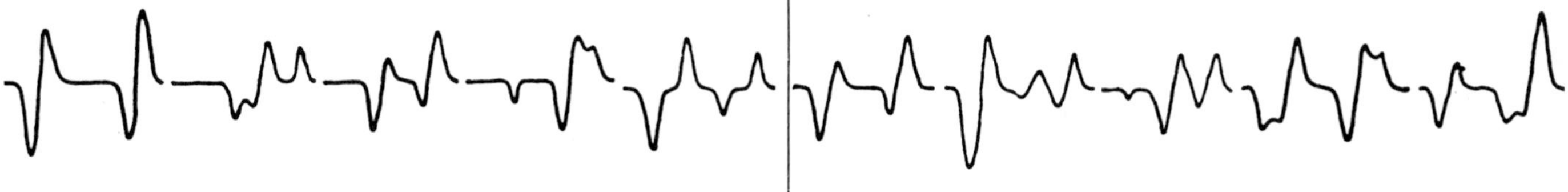

Numbers (2)

Incidentally, finding numbers in the urban landscape is very easy, and looking for them is good eye-sharpening exercise. I once made a slide show, a "countdown" from 100 to 0, and it took months. The hunt was more than satisfying and the reward was a new awareness of something previously invisible. The game, of course, is to find unexpected shapes, sizes and contexts. To play it with a minimum of frustration, it helps to have a long zoom lens or telephoto, plus a "macro" or close-up lens.

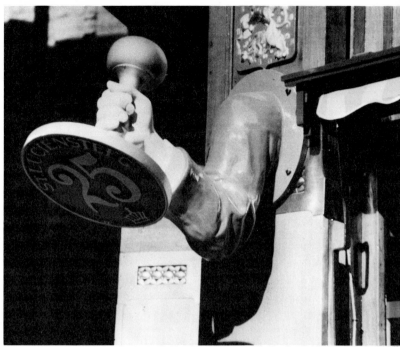

Art and Reality

(Seeing with the Mind)

Most people with seeing deficiencies — most modern people, in other words — prefer representational, "realistic" art to abstractions. In looking at a painting, if they can identify a horse, landscape or bowl of fruit, they are satisfied that they have "seen" it. It is "real."

We have here two pictures. The nude, a painting by Chabas, has been popular for generations. The other is an arrangement of flowing lines. It suffers in reproduction: in the original the lines are red, white and green against a background of deep orange and purple.

The question is, what do you think about these pictures?

- If you could have one or the other, which would you pick?
- What was your first fast reaction? Did you like one, both, or neither?
- Would you describe either as a "work of art"?
- Which picture is more "real"?
- Which, in your opinion, would bring a higher price if offered for sale?

Enough questions. Now turn the page.

I really shouldn't do this, but the photograph of the cars is the same view as the "abstraction" on page 21.

You can do it yourself by loading your camera with color film and taking a time exposure of night traffic. The car lights will become lines, and if you move the camera around during the exposure, or shake it, the results will be more interesting.

Now which picture is more "real," the abstraction, the nude, or the snapshot?

We have now a fourth picture, a painting by the late Jackson Pollock, and it too is an abstract arrangement of lines and colors.

- Does it look more or less "real" than the girl in the water?
- Would you accept it as a gift?
- What would it bring at an auction?
- Is it a "work of art"?
- What is a work of art?

23 | How to See

23 | How to See

Focus

We see what we are looking for, what we have been trained to see by habit or tradition. The notion that we come upon a scene and see everything has no truth in it. You can test this by looking hard at an unfamiliar room or a shop window for two minutes, which is a long time. Then turn away and check what you remember, whether items, shapes, colors.

Some people are reputed to have photographic memories, and perhaps they do. But the camera has another lesson for us: both photographs were taken with the camera in the same location, but the focus was changed. This is the way the eye-mind linkage works: if I am interested in Sweeney, I don't see the bird. And, of course, it works the other way too.

We see what interests us.

Arrows

The French artist Jean-Michel Folon once made a motor trip from Rome to Brescia, and counted the arrows en route. They came to well over a thousand. His print *Flight from the City* (see detail below) becomes comprehensible when one connects the artist's *doing* with his *seeing*.

There is no doubt that modern man has more arrows shot at him in the course of a weekend than were ever used in the most extravagant of the old Indian epics.

Arrows are part of the public baggage that goes with an addiction to mobility. They are a powerful, pervasive element in the modern scene. They prick, cajole, exhort, sell, direct; and there is no way of measuring the amount of brain damage they do. It comes for free, however, like air pollution, Muzak in elevators, and the gentle sound of police sirens.

I strongly urge a respectful emulation of Folon's arrow-counting trip to Brescia. I can guarantee that after four concentrated hours you will never be quite the same, ever again.

Nonverbal Messages

Every object in any environment may be considered a nonverbal message input, subject to decoding by any suitable receiver within range.

Here we have two such inputs, both pieces of the synthetic environment, both aimed at pedestrians and motorists for reasons of convenience or survival. Such messages are brutal in their simplicity, and they are meant to be read at speed. Technically they are no different from the sign showing a golden sun.

The important difference is that the sun is an invitation, and the very form and material of the sign are warm and inviting. The other examples have no time for charm and they usually consist of commands or prohibitions.

Informal Messages

Modern societies are an unending source of frustration for very large numbers of people in failing to provide for two-way communication. Messages out in the street tend to be prohibitions: no loitering, no spitting, no smoking, no parking, no admittance; or orders: go, stop, turn left, curb your dog, and so on. Radio and television are of necessity one-way, with the result that few citizens can find anyone to listen when they want to speak their minds.

Inevitably, individuals rebel in a variety of ways, ranging from vandalism to the writing of messages on public surfaces. Most of these are angry protests, probably by people pushed to the limits of endurance by the solitude, pressure and insecurity of existence which are so conspicuous a part of the contemporary scene.

Along with the displays of anger, there is endless evidence of a desire to escape anonymity through personal expression. Automobiles, for whatever reason, are favored objects for such creations. The graffiti in New York's subways, on the other hand, are almost always calligraphic rather than symbolic or directly decorative.

Those who deplore the defacing of public property might turn the problem around, and consider what motivates the defacers and how to provide suitable locations for their eruptions. This is not as difficult as it may seem, for there is in fact very little one could do in most center cities that would make them worse than they are.

NIXON HAS MET HIS FINISH IN THE MAD HOUSE

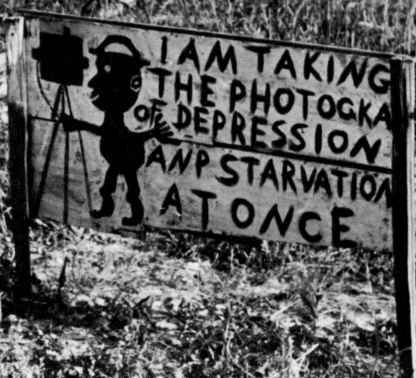

I AM TAKING THE PHOTOGKA OF DEPRESSION ANP STARVATION AT ONCE

Big Messages

Billboards have been around so long that we tend not to see what they do to their surroundings. The monster Winston ad raises a question: was the sign designed to fit the building, or was the building shaped to fit the sign? Whichever way we see it, there is an extraordinary difference in scale between the sign and the buildings nearby. Mary Quant does even more damage to an old shopping street in Copenhagen. The most astonishing thing about these erosions of visual space is that nobody notices.

Other billboards are entertaining for their content. The Marlboro Country ads, which seem to be very successful, offer an interesting example of brainwashing through fantasies. The Marlboro user presumably gets out of the subway or bus, jumps on his faithful steed, and gallops off into never-never land for an exhilarating nine-to-five day. Winston implies that anyone smoking this brand (in the box, please) is a handsome, hirsute stud, irresistible to women and invulnerable to emphysema.

"Only V.O. is V.O." is one of those fascinating statements which cannot be challenged no matter how you attack it. If V.O. isn't V.O., then what is it? This is a classic example of saying absolutely nothing with an air of unimpeachable authority.

The truck is something else again: without words it tells precisely what business Yale is in, and the 3-D sign, suspended in its improbable environment, has the slightly surrealistic quality of an oversized toy.

Billboards are the subject of controversy all over the country. Vermont has banned them. How do you feel about them, and about the freedom of private business to put them up wherever space is available?

Important Documents

Everyone, except for the totally dispossessed, has important documents. These have to do with birth and death, the right to drive a car, the awarding of high honors and valuable prizes, and, of course, the possession of negotiable equities like stocks, bonds, winning lottery tickets, and mortgages.

It is typical of such documents that they are executed in complicated and obsolete styles. Some of the complexity, like the borders of stock certificates, is designed to foil forgers, or at least to make their work unprofitable. The styles are obsolete because it is one of our peculiarities to attach more importance to old things than to new. Not all old things, to be sure. Few of us would want to go to Paris in Charles Lindbergh's plane. Just most old things. This is why we try to disguise a perfectly good all-electric kitchen as a Spanish *bodega*, buy station wagons with printed wood grain on the outside, pay a high premium to get a TV set in a Mediterranean or Provincial cabinet, or expect a higher tab in a roadside joint made up to look as if Charles Dickens had lunched there. A stock certificate all fussed up with curlicues and other engraved decoration smells of old money, and we all know that old money is better (higher social status, for one thing) than new money.

We also like obsolete styles because the past is dead, and hence contains no surprises. As modern people we know about surprises — that they are almost all bad. This is why certificates like those of Big Jim Consolidated Mining are comforting. We do not have to read the words: the design tells us almost everything we want to know.

In Saul Steinberg's magnificent spoof, a diploma to end all diplomas, we get the same visual message: Important Document. And it is just as well, too, for if we look closely we find there is not a single legible word in it.

Reinforced Messages

When someone puts up a sign on which words and a picture say the same thing, one wonders if this is not another example of the kind of overkill which has become so common in the urban landscape. It might be, in many instances, but I suspect that there are other reasons for it. One is that many signs, especially in the old cities, go back to preliterate days, when a restaurant, say, called the Black Cat would fail to get its message across unless there was a picture. Another reason has to do with a desire to make sure that people see the sign, so that the duplication of visual and verbal messages might be considered a fail-safe procedure: if one part of the message misses, perhaps the other will not.

Whatever the reasons, these signs, which seem to be more common in the old parts of center cities than elsewhere, contribute a fair amount of visual entertainment, for the pictures are usually produced by earnest amateurs. They invariably achieve legibility, but added to this is a primitive quality, not without its own charm, which we associate with painters like Rousseau and Grandma Moses.

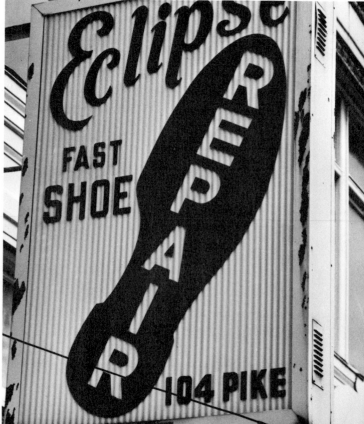

No-No

A favorite pastime of city administrators, police departments and those concerned with traffic is saying "no." Mostly these prohibitions are spelled out in words. There is also, however, an ancient tradition of nonverbal communication which is effective with less clutter. The range is very broad and rich, going from the nightmarish Berlin Wall to the almost comic pileup of street barriers. The visual spectrum includes the sharp warning to would-be sitters, a brutal "Keep Out" pattern on a castle entrance, improvised roadblocks to slow down park gate-crashers, a wonderfully delicate picket fence of the last century.

Art

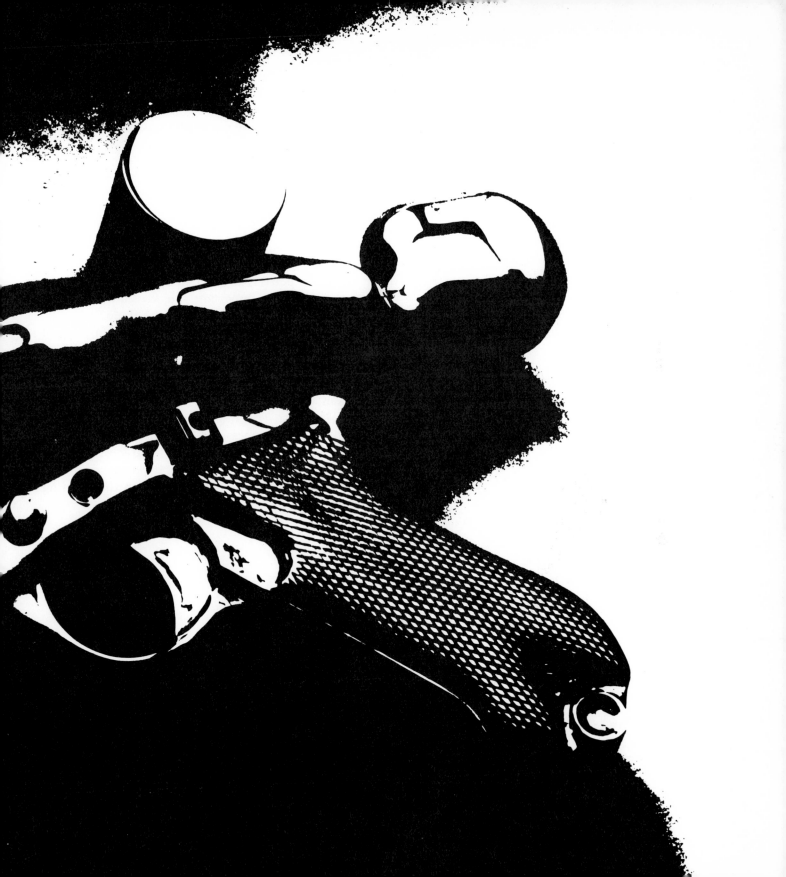

VIP Portraits

Item: one soup can, silk-screened on canvas. Artist, Andy Warhol. Date: 1964.

Item: one portrait of a young man, possibly Guidobaldo II, Duke of Urbino. Oil on wood. Artist, Bronzino, Florentine, 1503–1572.

Question: what do these two pictures have in common? (They are close to the same size, incidentally; about two feet by three). How and where does the elegant young aristocrat connect with the inelegant can?

Hypothesis: they are both portraits of important subjects. In the sixteenth century an important subject was a person; in the fading years of the twentieth century an important subject is a thing. Once everyone knew who the Duke of Urbino was; who can name the president, board chairman, largest stockholder of the soup company? But the can! Universally known. Worth at least $400 million a year in sales. Obviously worth a portrait.

Can the hypothesis be checked out? Is it right? Who knows? The important thing is to confront these silent messages, and let the thoughts, no matter how subversive, trickle into awareness. Do you have a different theory? The important thing to remember is that the trip is more fun than getting there.

Hero, Dragon, Lady

We have here examples that are pretty old hat: Saint George slays the dragon. Both maidens, toothsome, prayerful, passive, grateful, wait for their heroes to get on with the job. The dragon and the locomotive have fire in their vitals, belch smoke, and chase around devastating the countryside. In each version of the fable the male's virility is challenged symbolically. The women wait, like cows in a herd where the bulls are slugging it out. Each, beyond a doubt, will be more than pleased to pay the standard going rate for such services, which is fair enough considering the hero's risk, so clearly spelled out in the lower right corner of the painting.

To see in this way, the observer, as receiving set, has to know a little about Christian legend, a bit about the psychological reading of such tales. A receiver with a broader bandwidth would have some information about industrial engineering design in the later nineteenth century; to probe deeper he would need some familiarity with painting, with Sienese painting in the sixteenth century, with the composition of pictures, with the attitudes of painters to nature.

What we see is what we bring to the seeing.

Noble Beasts

When animals appear as bronze or stone effigies in public places, it is always possible that they are portraits, but not probable. The use of animals as symbols for qualities such as strength, piercing vision, courage, speed, and so on, is very old and it appears to be universal. Lions and eagles, as the top predators in their class, are seen on coins, government seals, flags. Their popularity is based on the simple fact that Man, top predator in *his* class, knows a real pro when he sees one. I have not yet encountered a hyena or jackal on a public monument, although, considering the nature and quality of recent Administrations, it might be worth reexamination.

Horses, as noble, high-spirited, faithful beasts, are popular as supports for local heroes. Horses with wings (Pegasus) are of course very special. The lion of Saint Mark also has wings.

Canada, a more civilized society than many, celebrates the native moose on its twenty-five-cent piece. While the moose does appear in U.S. public places, it never makes top billing, such as on a coin. Its sponsorship is usually local. Mexico has a ten-peso coin with an eagle (good) destroying a serpent (bad). All societies seem to have ambivalent feelings about snakes.

The strangled eagle, one of those shots the photographer dreams of, sits on a flagpole base in front of Washington's Union Station. There are four authentic American eagles per flagpole base and one offers its neck and beak to hold the lanyard from the flag flying high above.

Thus, to keep Old Glory flying, the vanishing American eagle has to submit to strangulation. It would all be a funny, funny picture and anecdote if it were not so close to the reality of an endangered species.

Public People and Nonpeople

Public sculpture is an outdoor mirror in which a society looks to see what it is: heroic, boastful, managerial, sentimental, or perhaps just in love with aluminum rivets. The most revealing thing about it is its demonstration of how the society spends its petty cash. The most useful thing about it, in many cases, is its ability to hold lots of pigeons. The most extraordinary thing about it has been the gradual vanishing of the human face and figure, frozen for the moment like the Cheshire cat's grin.

Henry Moore's family is a good sample: the man, woman and child are still there to be seen, but the forms are melting. Maillol's haunting, perfectly balanced beauties are perhaps the last and greatest before the photo floods went out. The Lipchitz totem (page 58) goes back to earlier, precandle days.

The Moore figures melt. Lipchitz finds fragments, a hand, an arm, assembles them not quite knowing what they are or where they come from. It doesn't matter, Lipchitz is a magician; in his hands three hot dogs and a car jack (God forbid) could become great sculpture. The same, in very different ways, goes for Moore and Calder. Dubuffet, on the other hand, makes large contorted white lumps and then paints them with thick lines (see page 58), creating the impression that he is trying to remember what people (or is it trees?) look like and not quite making it.

In any case, the people are out and the geometrics are in: shining doughnut holes escaping from square doughnuts, teetering cubes, cylinders whittled out like old organ pipes. It is a cool, pseudo-mathematical world, not unlike the bureaucracies themselves, where employees at all levels are given the choice (never said out loud) of excommunication or conformity to management's dream of the perfect cyborg.

The twentieth century is the first in human history that may end with no image of man in its inventory of creations.

Symbolic People

One can tell a good bit about how a society sees itself by looking at its self-images. Sometimes these are major paintings, often cartoons (Colonel Blimp, John Bull, Mickey Mouse). Mickey did not slip in by mistake: Erich Fromm identifies him as an accurate psychological portrait of the average American.

Uncle Sam, more popular during World War I than recently, is past draft age, pure Wasp, middle income, a joiner. Like so many of our creations he has been commercialized and is currently doing his bit to improve the sales of pizzas, heroes and other products.

Liberty Leading the People by Delacroix is one of the most widely reproduced symbolic figures. Her vigor, bursting femininity and assured way of taking charge of things identify her as unmistakably French.

The Church is so huge an institution that it functions like a society. The roster of saints as symbols is enormous, and they are generally identified by accessories, such as the keys of Saint Peter, the staff and Child of Saint Christopher, and the arrows of Saint Sebastian, who is shown here in a fifteenth-century Italian version, bristling with arrows and impassive as a pincushion.

Cyborgs

Here we have some beautifully finished pieces of sculpture which look like people. But only up to a point, for they are all faceless, armless and sexless. Furthermore, each seems to be surgically connected with machines or instruments. They only seem strange because we do not think about the number of people going around with pacemakers, plastic arteries, or prosthetic devices, or connected to dialysis machines. There must also be many people who feel, when out of their cars, as if a part of their body were missing.

In a certain sense, then, the images presented by these seeming fantasies are very close to everyday reality.

The new name for these people-machine composites is cyborgs, but the idea is very old: mythologies are full of winged horses, fire-breathing creatures, centaurs, mermaids, gods with goat's feet.

To produce figures so strange, and yet so nightmarish in their familiarity, executed at so high a level of perfection, takes an artist of rare quality. The sculptor's name is Ernest Trova.

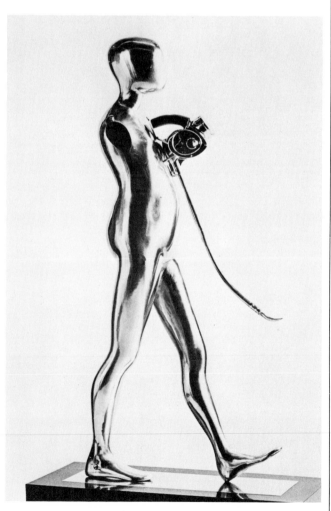

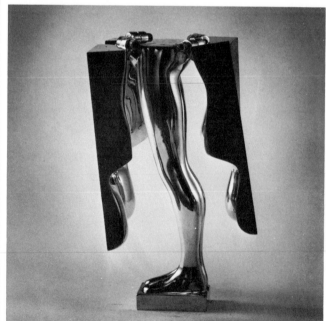

City Walls

The rash of wall painting that has swept through the entire world in the past half-dozen years or more produces visual images that are generally as large or larger than billboards. And yet there is a difference. Despite their size and conspicuous locations, despite the extreme difference in scale between the walls and the building elements, like windows and fire escapes, associated with them, there is no indication of public resistance comparable to the widespread opposition to billboards. One wonders why. Is a billboard visual pollution while a wall painting — even a bad one — is not? What triggered these outdoor paintings, anyway? Many show a considerable investment of time and materials if not money.

One can understand the artists' point of view: here is a large-scale opportunity to make a meaningful (to the artist) statement. Generally speaking, industrial societies have little use for artists, except for the kitsch manufacturers, and it is frustrating not to be needed. But still, someone has to pay for these walls. What are the clients — landlords, one would assume — after?

The categories into which these paintings fall include protest (most often in slum areas); abstractions, in public spaces like playgrounds and miniparks, which the controlling bureaucracy favors because they are noncontroversial; and commercial messages like the music wall (on a music store) in Minneapolis. Corporations also like abstractions for the same reason as municipal bureaucracies.

My guess about the popularity of painted city walls is that they are a kind of outlet for the frustrations caused by the steadily deteriorating urban environment, that everyone likes them as colorful accents in a drab urban setting, but mainly because they are honest and personal. The billboards are neither, as a rule, and the fact that they have to be duplicated in one location after another sets up both

boredom and resentment, at least in those who are able to see them. Graffiti are different, for neither are they organized, like a painting, nor do they contain any message beyond the expression of a desire to see one's name in a public place.

Double Takes

The double take is a trick used by merchants, makers of chocolate cigarettes, pranksters, Dadaist and Surrealist artists.

The American flag, modified by an angry critic, has shock value because, at first glance, one fails to see the dollar signs replacing the familiar stars.

Man Ray's iron of 1921 still retains its impact, creating a physical reaction almost like scratching a fingernail on a blackboard.

The photomontages of Hans Hollein and Claes Oldenburg expose more levels of meaning. Can an aircraft carrier, with its superexpensive air-conditioned accommodation for 6,000 to 10,000 men be reused as a town? Would it work? What would a town built for one-quarter the price be like? Why do the aircraft carriers (etc., etc.) always get the money?

One really does a double take when confronted by Hollein's Rolls Royce radiator growing in the financial district of New York. Do we see a natural affinity between the Rolls and Wall Street? Is the radiator, with its vertical metal fins, virtually indistinguishable from the new buildings, telling us something about modern buildings and modern products, both equally devoid of character? There are recent high-rise buildings that show more than a passing resemblance to the surveyor's transit, here seen as a rural monument (page 70).

A different impression is conveyed by Hollein's turbine, half buried in lower Manhattan like an archaeological relic from some science fiction future. Are artists implying that the monstrous scale of these artifacts is more appropriate for the modern city than the pedestrian-scale city blocks? Oldenburg's huge toilet floats raise the same question, except that there is also a hint that the water in the Thames is not that different from the water in a toilet.

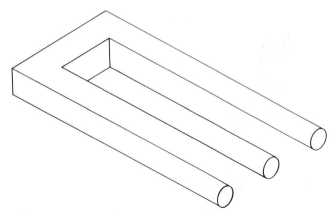

If you feel that these images are exaggerated, an aerial view of an expressway and its interchanges tells the identical story. Almost any view of the U.S. city is a double take, if we bother to look for it. The delight in deception is as old as the race: the conjurer who makes an elephant disappear off a stage or pulls playing cards out of people's ears; the set designer who transports us from a theater into a different world. When the laws of perspective were discovered, architects and artists of the Renaissance entertained themselves and their public with painted domes that were really flat, painted windows that were not there.

In recent years, as researchers have turned to studies of the brain and the ways in which we see things, "impossible figures," such as the ones shown here, were found to have value in revealing how we see.

For us, who are neither artists nor scientific researchers for the most part, the great value of such drawings is that they prove beyond any doubt that more of our seeing goes on in the brain than in our eyes.

We look at the well-known drawing by Escher, showing a canal and a wheel being turned by a waterfall, and, while the building is very odd indeed, what is going on seems perfectly normal. It is not until we try to figure out how the water gets from the bottom of the fall to the top that we have to discredit the evidence of our eyes. The water does indeed get from the bottom to the top, but in defiance of all the laws of gravity. It takes a distinct mental effort to realize that we have been tricked by the artist.

The other figures, also widely used in books on perception and illusion, are similar: each looks perfectly ordinary at first glance, but there is no possible way that either could be made.

Transformations

An aluminum can with a soft drink in it costs, these days, thirty or thirty-five cents before sales tax. The same can, empty, brings around one-half cent at the reclamation centers.

If the can is thrown away after use, in the great U.S. tradition of littering whatever landscape is within reach, and then run over by a truck, you get a small piece of junk, familiar to anyone exposed to cans and trucks.

There is something else to see, however: the transformation of a shiny cylinder into a kind of accidental sculpture. With time and the passage of a number of vehicles, the metamorphosis goes on until the can is completely flattened out, its surface now a dirty but still visually interesting rough texture.

The crushed can and the mutilated statue are alike in that each has been modified by collision with another physical reality. The ancients produced a substantial amount of sculpture, much of it subsequently mutilated; we produce cans. The message of the statue is that the essence of a beautiful thing can survive a surprising amount of damage.

All automobile graveyards are full of extraordinary transformations, some nightmarish, but all of them dramatic. I once made a film in one of these places and it was disturbing to discover that Detroit's bland and shiny products are more "alive" visually in death than when they come off the assembly lines.

Junk is the most pervasive product of technological society. There is little or no junk visible in backward countries, for everything is cannibalized, cleaned, reused, sold. One might say, with a reasonable probability of being right, that come war or peace, affluence or depression, junk is our ultimate landscape.

Many artists have been fascinated by junk and by the inexhaustible richness of forms it assumes. Ar-

tists have been painting landscapes for centuries, and if ours fills up with junk, junk is what they paint. Artists always know where the action is.

Junk, like they say in the commercials, is the real thing. We can look at the chilling photograph of a burning dump near Moab, Utah, and marvel at the apocalyptic scale of the devastation, accomplished without a single nuclear explosion through nothing more than the cooperative efforts of uncounted dedicated consumers. The photographer has shown us a familiar scene, but he has also produced a powerful symbol of aspects of modern life we generally choose not to see.

And what do the artists do with the junk we all make? Why, they look at it, sniff it, take it home, play with it, create little junk worlds just like the real one, and maybe sell it to collectors or museums.

Junk is not just the disorder of discards. It, like everything else, can be read on a variety of levels. At the most immediate and superficial, it is unsightly waste which immobilizes land that could be put to better use; it is unsanitary and pollutes streams. When burned (the most common type of disposal) it pollutes the air as well. Communities, conscious of health and the tax base, try to control location and disposal methods. At another level, junk is a resource that becomes more valuable as prime mineral sources are depleted. The same holds for garbage, a kind of organic junk, and cities are beginning to compost it on an increasing scale, or burn it for fuel. At still another level, junk can be seen as an unexpected source of accidental beauty. It can be studied, as by archaeologists, to get a better insight into the nature of a society. It can be seen as a symbol of

social values, and here the readings can vary all over the lot, for the beholder always brings with him a good part of what he sees.

Consider this: junk is an expression of a death-obsessed society, feverishly cramming everything it can buy or steal into its insatiable maw in a frantic effort to fill an inner emptiness that fails to respond to a diet of consumer products. It is social excrement that now covers the planet, poisons the environment, and pollutes the oceans. Such a view is by no means uncommon among writers and critics, but one suspects that unless one felt this despairing about our present and future, this is not what one would see. What view would be seen by a paid apologist for the oil companies? Would a conventional politician, absorbed in manufacturing new promises, find it expedient to present such an opinion?

One might also turn to nature for hints on what to see. Nature, through avalanches, hurricanes, forest fires, disease, droughts, earthquakes, tidal waves and volcanic eruptions, produces unsightly messes all the time and occasionally on a very large scale. The messes are made up of organic and inorganic materials. Yet we never think of the natural environment as a repository for nature's litter, for the reason that everything is eventually recycled. If one can wait long enough, lava turns into good soil, burned forests are covered with new vegetation, and so on. Junk, as a human and industrial equivalent, is also a normal consequence of activity, and if nature's model were followed we would recycle it without even thinking about it. This is what we are almost certain to be doing, out of necessity or, better, from a new sense of proper planetary behavior, in less than a half century.

In the meantime, it provides some extraordinarily interesting activity for anyone who enjoys the pleasures of seeing. If you have never gone through a large junkyard, it is a strange, out-of-the-world experience. There is poignancy in these transformed relics of technology. They have a startling power to evoke images of human use and ephemeral dreams of affluence. It may well be that artists turn to junk as a raw material from time to time because this is the only moment in modern life when a consumer product relates directly, intimately and deeply to the human condition.

That ancient Chevy grille: what a host of associations . . . a mining robot from the asteroid belt, a Baltic knight in Eisenstein's *Alexander Nevsky*.

The station wagon, gradually becoming one with the desert, created by some anonymous Georgia O'Keeffe weary of painting bleached skulls. . . . The

79

junk joke, a chromium-plated horse and rider, composed of bumpers and other polished car parts. . . . The bicyclelike fragment by Jean Tinguely, part of a large junk machine which destroyed itself at a museum garden party in 1960.

It is hard to imagine junk art without the automobile as its major patron, so to speak. The "art" work on the left was found near New York's old Fulton Fish Market on a fine Sunday morning. Everything was in exactly the right place: textured asphalt, white line and tire tread. A click of the shutter and lo! another piece of instant art.

Strobe

"The artist," Ben Shahn once remarked, "is a person who solves problems before others are aware that they exist." Here is a case in point. It has to do with the question of who sees what when.

Dog on a Leash was painted in 1912 by the Italian Futurist Giacomo Balla. The problem he saw was how to paint a body in motion. This is what he did. The critics divided themselves into two groups — those who thought Balla had gone over the brink, and those who felt that his efforts to attract attention had gone too far.

The photograph shows a body in motion, lighted by stroboscopic flash. The process was invented by Harold Edgerton in 1938 and opened a new view of reality.

Moral: if you ever hear critics arguing about the sanity of a new painter, buy his paintings. It is better to be in the company of a crazy painter than a sane critic.

Old Stuff

Clocks

To see a clock is to sense the accelerating tempo of social existence. Church bells, the muezzins' call to prayer, sundials, tower clocks, mantel clocks, wristwatches and now the digitals.

As time gets sliced thinner, we do less with it, waiting in traffic jams, in checkout lines, trying to get phone calls through.

The less we do with time, the more watches we buy if only to count the minutes we are losing.

The more watches we buy, the fewer public clocks are installed.

We lose not only urban ornaments, but valuable place markers to help orient us; and another expression of civic pride.

Hydrants

The Oxford dictionary puts a date of 1828 on the word, and gives it a U.S. origin. It certainly looks both nineteenth-century and American: functional, gutsy, no-nonsense.

There are people who collect things like fire hydrants and manhole covers on film, and I am one of them. We find these cumbersome artifacts charming in that they look exactly like what they do and what they are made of. In other words, they show an economy both rare and refreshing.

Furthermore, while the variety of shapes and sizes is endless (which uses up a lot of film), the basic uniformity of the design concept never changes.

Gingerbread

One of the really powerful arguments for the unity of mankind is gingerbread.

Take any human individual anywhere, give him a dwelling made of wood planks, provide him with a drill and a jigsaw, and go away. When you come back, and it doesn't matter where, this is what you will find. These few samples, originally photographed with nothing special in mind, were taken in Trinidad, eastern Long Island, Tbilisi in the U.S.S.R., Colorado.

They could have been taken in any of 6,500 other locations. The moral is simple, and clear: no race that spends this much time and energy cutting shapes into wood planks can be all bad.

Industrial Romance

We can look at these antiques with an indulgent smile at the advertising naiveté of yesteryear, or we can go past the expressions of fashion and try to see what has happened to the people who create advertising in the last half century.

The earliest examples are very low-pressure: the little girl and the baby carriage; the listening dog; the clean-cut American girl telephone operator; a seductive homebody caressing the General Electric portable grill of 1908; plump virginity driving a 1913 Evinrude outboard. It's all gentle, gemütlich, homey, and tries to persuade through association with images of dogs, children, superrespectable young women. They are basically testimonial ads, although those testifying are paid models.

If this were a history rather than a series of quick looks, we would find that what really happened over these fifty years was a progression from persuasion to mass manipulation, using fantasy, insecurity, social or money ambitions as the instruments. With this comes a new kind of language, absolutely papal in tone, but saturated in a kind of ambiguity that lobotomizes the listener. From "The Pause That Refreshes," a fair enough claim for a soda pop, Coca-Cola goes to "It's the Real Thing." Since all such communications are rigidly one-way, no one can even ask what is real about what thing. Somehow a sweet carbonated drink becomes a way of life.

We can compare the girl advertising Michelin tires with her granddaughter on the BMW 900: one is arty titillation for an overdressed period, the other suggests that if you, lucky fellow, owned a BMW 900, this desirable young woman would find you at least as much of a turn-on as your motorcycle.

ou work
with
smile

Drink
Coca-Cola
TRADE MARK
Delicious and Refreshing

after
the pause that refreshes

Mobility

Going Places

In the man-made environment, everything flows — water, sewage, people, vehicles, energy.

Scenes of movement, and the architecture sheltering it, fall into two categories: those where the movement is smooth, unimpeded, strike us as agreeable, attractive, appropriate, exciting, beautiful. Those places where traffic is clogged, where travelers wait in discomfort, where the design is full of visual impediments provoke feelings ranging from distaste to hysteria.

Both airport corridors (page 105) were designed by architects: one could see, the other could not. The way to judge the relative quality of the design is to imagine walking through one, and then the other. At least 90 percent of U.S. air terminals are monuments to clutter.

A license to practice architecture (granted by boards of visual illiterates) is no protection, alas, against visual pollution.

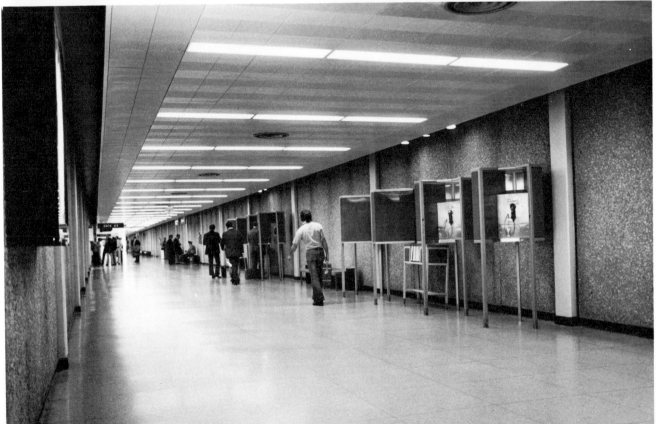

Pedestrian Streets

The growth of pedestrian streets and malls the world over is following an exponential curve. In America, and no doubt elsewhere, it has become a mark of status: a city without at least one pedestrian street can no longer think of itself as "progressive."

While fashions in urban design can be as silly as fashions in other spheres, the popularity of the pedestrian street is soundly based on the simple fact that it is more pleasant to use: it carries fewer exhaust fumes, it is less noisy, and walking is not regimented by auto traffic and stop-and-go lights.

The quality of pedestrian malls varies all over the place, starting with an ordinary street closed to traffic, such as the street in New Orleans' French Quarter (page 107), going on to streets in formerly derelict areas where a few portable planters begin to make their appearance, to total projects such as the fabulous Fussgängerbereit in Munich, where nothing has been omitted that might make the use of the area more pleasant (see page 108).

Then, of course, there are always the narrow, sometimes steep streets in old towns where even a minicar would have trouble squeezing through.

Not all pedestrian streets are "pure" in the sense that all other traffic is excluded. In Zurich's famous Bahnhofstrasse the cars have been eliminated, but the immaculate silent streetcars still go through. Nicollet Mall in Minneapolis (page 107) has an ingenious serpentine street which permits buses, police cars and fire trucks to go through. These "mixed" streets are sometimes more interesting, visually and in actual use, probably because of the differences in scale and speed.

There are two things to watch for in pedestrian malls: the faces and body movements of the people using them, and the types and quality of the street furniture installed to intensify the new character of the street as a space for easy walking, sitting and socializing.

Public Sitting

Sitting around in public places, watching other people go by, must be the world's most popular inactivity, and by a big margin. It costs nothing, requires no expensive equipment, and there is never a dull moment.

The best places for sitting are, almost without exception, places designed primarily for some other purpose, and of all the possible sites and situations, stairs are at the top of anyone's list. Stairs offer changes of level and thus an overview of whatever there is to view; stairs are at the very beginning of theater.

Looking at planned seating, one of the best examples is the Swiss promenade (opposite), with pedestrians in the road and benches under thick leaf cover, their backs to the road, facing waterfront activity.

Outdoor sitting brings out the contortionist in all of us: just changing positions from time to time in the search for total comfort can profitably occupy an entire summer afternoon.

Corporate sitting, like so many things corporate, is regimented, antihuman in concept, mediocre and boring.

The most ancient form of enhanced inactivity is having your shoes shined. South of the border, where this is raised to the level of communal art, the endlessly shifting relationship of the somnolent, sagging torso and the deft, birdlike movements of the young operative is minidrama in itself and dynamic public sculpture as well.

Even where benches are provided, sophisticated sitters are as likely to ignore them as not, and where no benches exist, lawns are just as good or better.

City Floors

As the topless high-rise office blocks keep crowding into decaying city centers, the need for some visual relief for pedestrians mounts. Since there is no usable surface left except pavements, this is where the action is.

The steady expansion of pedestrian malls has accelerated the growth of interest in the appearance and texture of the city's floor. Blind as the average citizen is, he can still see better than his car.

Manhole Covers

The humble manhole cover, as common and as invisible an element in the urban scene as the fire hydrant, was discovered as an art object by artists and designers some years ago. Since then there have been photo exhibits and at least one book of rubbings dealing with them.

The artist or designer looks at them and sees cast iron used with perfect appropriateness. The iron is cast into sand molds, which means that detail cannot be too fine. The design is functional in that the lettering and ornaments identify the maker, and, because the parts to be read are raised, traffic wear keeps polishing the design. Thus the manhole cover can be full of mud and remain legible. It also lasts practically forever and gets better with age.

Most manhole covers are circular, for obvious reasons; a few have other shapes; not all are big enough to let a man through but keep the name anyway. Variations on the theme are without limit, and as far as I know, the design is used all over the world. The reason is simply that no one has ever come up with anything better.

Erosion of Pedestrian Space

In most of the battles between man and the machine, the latter continues to win, despite the growing number of pedestrian malls.

One of the common forms of erosion comes from street widening. In the small German town of Überlingen, we can see two forms: reduction of sidewalk space to the point where only a single person can make it between curb and steps and, farther down the street, the use of sidewalks for parking.

A subtler form of invasion is due to car overhangs. Their wheels rest legally against the curb, but the car keeps on going. In such cases, nobody talks about what is really happening, because business has an insatiable appetite for parking space. The only reason the Grand Canyon survives is that no one has found a commercial use for it.

Pismo Beach

I remember as a child looking at my father's *National Geographic*, marveling at the swarms of pilgrims bathing in the Ganges, packed body-to-body as far as the eye could reach. How could they survive? Could they escape? Where did they eat and sleep? And later there was Coney Island.

Now California, always first with the oldest as well as the newest, is about to find out. The new pilgrims — swollen beyond recognition in their synthetic carapaces: vans, pickups, beach buggies, campers, trailers, motor homes — come to land's end, bringing their own smog with them.

Who are they, refugees from San Fernando Valley? Squatters? Nature lovers? Lemmings?

There is very much of a muchness here, a lot of everything except beach. Do they like this kind of togetherness, or did some kind of hidden compulsion bring them here? What will happen by 2001, when everything we see in the picture will have at least doubled?

What would you like to bet that every third bumper has the sticker "Let's Keep America Beautiful"?

Bridges

Of all the structures and machines used for going places, the bridge is unique. Unlike the road, an earthbound strip, the bridge leaps, taking imagination with it. Like the plane, it defies gravity, but noiselessly. It "moves" with infinite grace without going anywhere. It never causes visual pollution; it soars across rivers and chasms, enhancing natural environments. The names of the great bridge builders are remembered.

The beauty of bridges, as we perceive the best of them, is related to the fact that they are a single-purpose design, and that all of their components are directly related to this one purpose. Everyone understands what a bridge is and does. The same is true of aqueducts.

Technology, while continually refining bridge design, has little effect on our response: the Pont-du-Gard (pages 130–131), built by the Romans a thousand years ago, is as satisfying an ornament in the French landscape today as it ever was.

The greatest artist-engineer in modern bridge design was Robert Maillart, a Swiss. The reason his work is so widely admired is his original use of concrete, in the form of slabs or plates rather than posts, and his total unity of expression, a model of elegance and economy of means (see page 133).

One of the silliest projects in modern times was the transplanting of London Bridge to the Arizona desert, a feat possible only for people lacking any connection with reality. Bridges exist only *in relation* to environments, never as monuments in isolation. Shipping London Bridge to a U.S. desert is like presenting a bracelet to a basket case.

Geometrics and
Other Exercises

Spirals

Spirals occur all through nature, and range in size from galaxies down to minute marine organisms. The Old Greeks were fascinated by spirals, incorporated them in their Ionic column, and developed mathematical rules for their behavior. If you grow beans or poison ivy, the counter-clockwise spiral quickly becomes visible as they climb. The chambered nautilus is an equiangular type of spiral, one which constantly expands as the outer surface rotates. Most galaxies are equiangular spirals, but nobody knows why.

Man-made spirals are fewer in number, and are often seen as systems for putting a straight line into a more compact form, such as spiral staircases, paper clips, bolts and screws.

The Swiss watch industry appears to be based in part on studies (made, appropriately, by Swiss mathematicians) of watch springs, which are also spirals. Now that the digital watches are moving in, maybe it won't matter much longer. Hurricanes, however, which will continue to matter for some time to come, are also spirals.

Circles

Looking for geometric forms is another agreeable exercise for the eyes, and circles are easy to find. Beer cans, tires, manholes, eyes, buttons, flowers, tree rings, traffic lights, doorknobs — you can make a long list without trying very hard.

The circle as a symbol has a prodigious history, connected with magic, religion, mythology, town planning. It means completeness, unity, the center of everything. The yin-yang symbol encloses all good and evil, interlocked within a circle. The sun and moon are circles. Anyone can draw a circle: all that is needed is a compass.

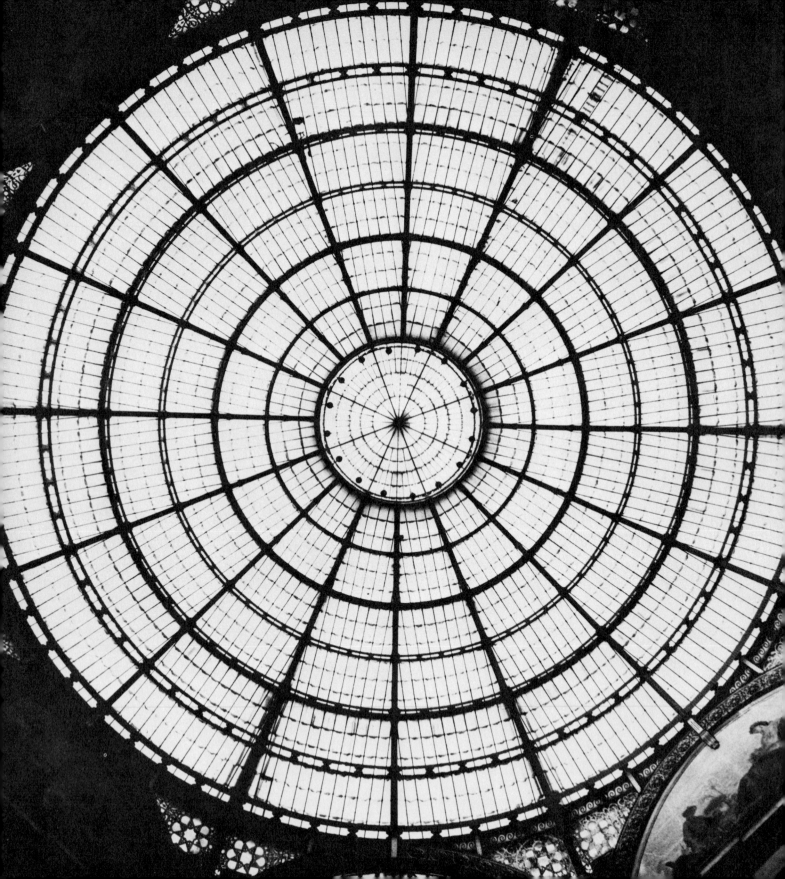

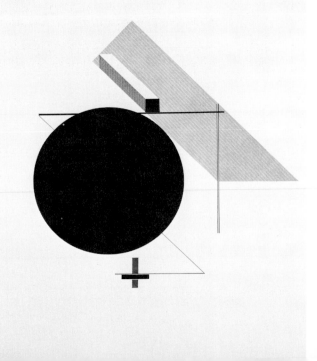

Patterns

Trying to deal with patterns in a few pages is like bailing out a boat with a teaspoon. Patterns are everywhere; they emerge in the eyepiece of an electron microscope and get recorded by cameras in satellites.

For reasons that are probably far from simple, we all get enormous pleasure out of patterns, possibly because they illustrate so beautifully the way the extremes of human perception — unity and diversity — flow together to make one thing. Patterns fascinate us the way people do: a million snowflakes are all alike and all different.

Patterns are dynamic and static. A flight of planes in formation never stays quite the same; contour-plowed land changes from season to season; sand dunes with their transparent shadows are constantly shifting with the wind, like clouds; a building in construction is a constantly changing pattern until it is completed.

Patterns are one of our best sources of information about the world. We can tell the age of a city, roughly, by the pattern of buildings and open spaces seen from the air, and the condition of crops photographed from satellites can be accurately appraised. Photography, in fact, has enormously enriched our awareness of patterns and their meanings.

The best way to find patterns is to go looking for them with a camera, and they are as plentiful in towns as in the country: shadows of fire escapes, back alleys, manhole covers, markings on streets, windows in large buildings, a row of brownstone houses . . .

Soft and Hard

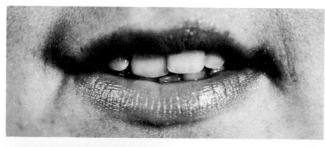

We have already noted that most modern people are visually crippled, partly by the so-called educational process, but also by the overload of visual stimuli in the urban environment. When one has a broken leg, one needs crutches to walk. Here we have one of a large series of such temporary assists, useful to anyone who wants to sharpen his perceptions.

The "crutch" is nothing more than a category of things, shapes or qualities. We currently have in our office the problem of designing a standard front for a chain of some four hundred shops. As a result, we are looking at shop fronts with an intensity we did not feel before. All real seeing is triggered by interest.

One example of an arbitrarily chosen exercise is to look for hardness and softness and the contrasts between these two qualities. Isolating the qualities of hard and soft gets us to look in a special way.

So suddenly we see: soft lips, hard teeth; soft flag, hard buildings; and so on. We also note transformations: the blimp and plastic greenhouse are soft until rigidified by air or gas pressure. The manhole cover, made of cast iron, was once liquid and then solidified after it was poured into the mold. The foam chair went from liquid to soft.

Claes Oldenburg's soft fan is a special exercise: because he took a familiar hard object and magnified it in soft materials, we are forced to see it with fresh eyes.

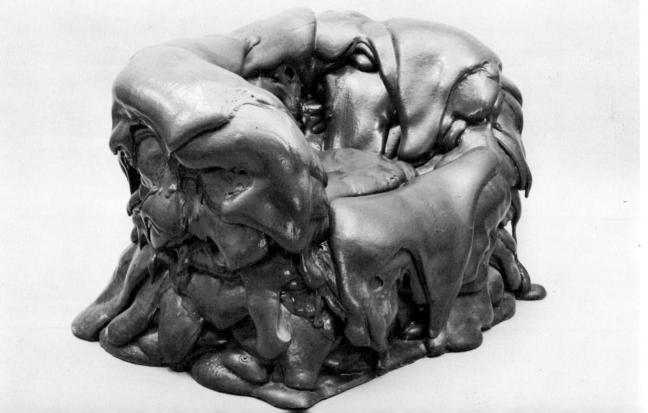

Traces and Tracks

For these, one generally has to get away from the hard surfaces of cities. Once in the world of earth, mud and sand, the traces of birds, trucks, shoes, boots and grasses are there.

A blade of beach grass becomes a wind-powered compass, making circles on the dunes; the imprint of a common rubber sole becomes a mysterious seal; birds leave their marks for the naturalists to read; tires churn up mud to create mini-airviews of unfamiliar water worlds.

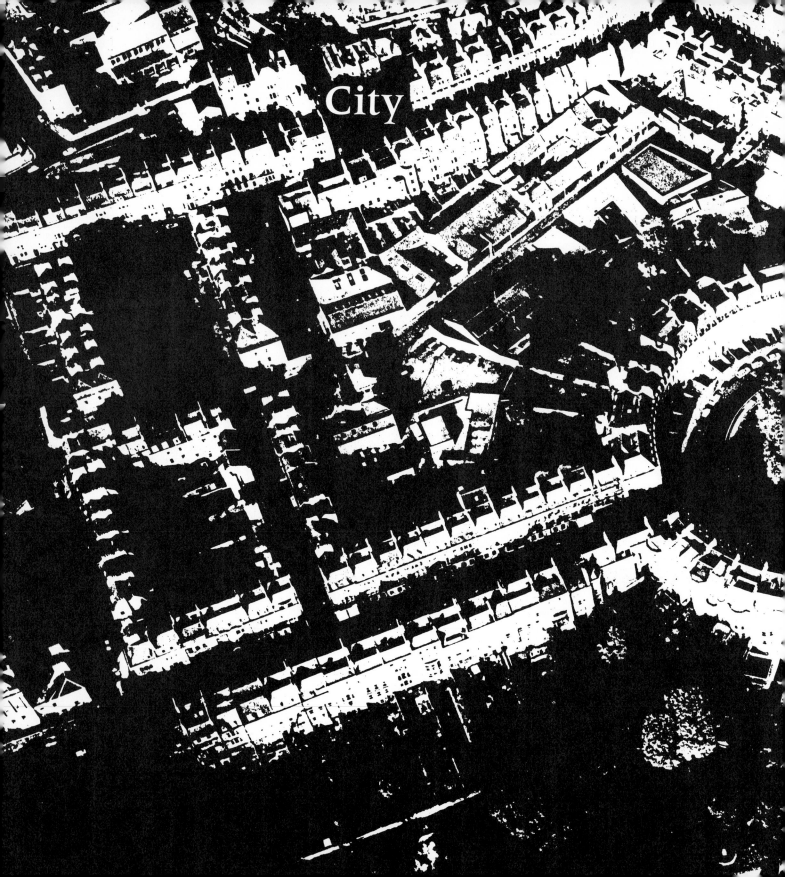

City

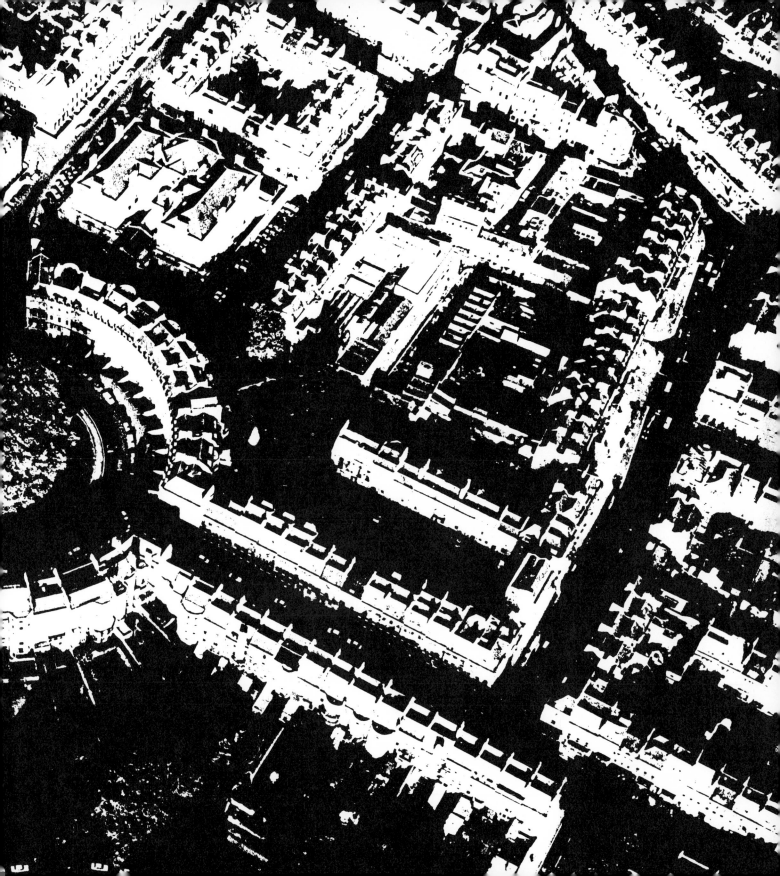

Great American Street Corner

A street corner is where well-behaved people cross the street. It would be a good place for a clear view of what might be happening. It is one of the places a city can put its best foot forward, so to speak.

This is not quite the way we tackle this interesting problem. Here we have two poles, a parking meter and a fire hydrant sprouting from the sidewalk. There is also a long-suffering tree and a tilted mailbox. Some of the information is legible, some isn't. The map of the neighborhood might have some information for the motorist, but it is doubtful. One pole, installed at a probable minimum cost of five hundred dollars, carries only two signs, both dealing with parking. Other civic ornaments on the corner include a street name, a one-way sign, an exhortation about emergency vehicles, some traffic lights. If you look carefully, you can find the place to cross.

This is *one* street corner. Most intersections have *four* corners. What do you suppose it costs to equip *one* intersection, remembering that most municipal projects probably cost three times (at least) real value, what with bureaucratic overstaffing and kickbacks? There no doubt are cities run with some degree of efficiency and honesty, but it is not likely that New York, where these photographs were taken, fits into this fortunate category.

The average taxpayer rarely expects to get value for his money, and the street corner is a prime example, not only of waste, but of "design overkill" as well, a kind of visual pigsty which pollutes the air around it for a fair distance. The taxpayer is thus cheated twice: once out of his money, and then out of an attractive city, by the visual cripples who put it together.

Why do they put in *two* expensive poles, one of which does almost nothing? Probably because two departments are involved, and they never talk to each other. Who dreamed up the useless, illegible map? Who figured out the location of the fire hydrant and mailbox? Nobody. Why does this municipal garbage crowd the street corner so unpleasantly?

Not known. Who is in charge of coordinating the design of street corners? Nobody at all. Is this how the whole city was put together? No. Only about 98 percent of it.

Does anyone ever notice a street corner, judge it in terms of decency, effectiveness, amenity? I don't know. Have you ever really looked at one?

Skylines

City skylines go from richly varied, idiosyncratic and sculptural to clusters of topless high-rise slabs.

In looking at such panoramas, one's personal values affect the seeing. If you believe that one reason for cities is the delight and enlightenment of their inhabitants, you may decide that an oversupply of corporate-ego-inflating towers is not a cause for rejoicing.

What you see may be what you get, but what you see is also what you think. In trying to "read" what the photos show, it helps a lot to note the functions of towers before and after, say, 1900.

Here we find, in the near total shift from churches, university, and government towers to office blocks, complete visual evidence that God is indeed dead.

But don't be too hasty in blaming capitalist greed. The new skyline is no different in Moscow, Novosibirsk or Belgrade.

Strips

The strip is a result of universal car ownership, the easy accessibility of relatively cheap land, and a widespread blindness which effectively prevents citizens and governing bodies from seeing what these uncontrolled commercial pileups do to their surroundings.

A strip, to isolate its peculiar qualities, has to be on a heavily traveled street or road with direct car access and a modicum of parking. It generally consists of cheaply built one-story structures and expensive signs. The scene is one of unrestrained competition and finally, in a fully developed strip, the dog-eat-dog behavior it so accurately portrays reaches a point where the signs and billboards cancel each other out.

At this stage the original purpose is blanked out and what we are left with is an incredibly expensive collective work of pop art. The place to see this in all its final, insane glory is Las Vegas, which is not really a city in the familiar sense but a random assortment of casinos, hotels, dwellings, office buildings and parking lots attached to roadside strips. There is no place on the North American continent that so powerfully symbolizes the American Dream of unending motion and of getting something for nothing.

Big Spaces

Everyone, except for a few with special phobias, has historically enjoyed big spaces. Roman baths, Byzantine churches, Gothic cathedrals, railroad terminals, *gallerias* are perennially popular with both local people and tourists.

Very big spaces became attainable in the mid-1800s, when the use of iron and steel, often combined with glass, suddenly made superspans possible. In the mid-1900s another leap was taken with air-supported structures and buildings with suspension roofs. It then became possible to build domes covering a square mile or more, with no supporting columns in the middle at all.

When looking at such spaces, it helps to see them better if we apply our familiar "levels of meaning" approach. Take the great old Galleria in Milan: why would anyone build it? Well, it is right alongside the big cathedral square. It rains quite a lot in Milan. It also gets very hot in the summer. If you make two streets in the form of a cross, pave the floor with mosaics, fill the buildings with shops and cafés at ground level, and throw two glass vaults over the streets, pleasant things happen.

Is that the only reason they built it, to keep the rain off and the summer heat out? No. It is also a monument to a king. Anything else? People, including architects and engineers, were excited by the new metal and glass structures. Is that all? No. It was an expression of civic and national pride, a focal point for the people of Milan. Was it a good investment? It all depends on which value system you use. Any nonverbal messages? Quite a few: exuberance, enjoyment, pride, celebration — all things we have run out of in the twentieth century.

Since modern society gives the general impression of an endless succession of identity crises, we might see what we can find in contemporary public spaces. Maybe it will help us to find out who we are. Let's try a visual comparison between the old Pennsylvania Station (now torn down to make way for some expensive mediocrity in the form of an office build-

ing and sports arena) and a recently built air terminal.

The old station was a bustling, echoing place closed in by lacy ironwork and glass. The glass was washed rarely, if ever, and the coating of grime way up in the air softened the light. It was a soaring monument to a total faith in the virtues of mobility and the achievements of building technology.

By comparison take the Newark air terminal, which is not the greatest of its kind, but certainly a long way from the worst. What does it signify, glorify, symbolize or commemorate? One would think that the messages from Penn Station would be amplified, for planes are much better than steam locomotives — they take us far more quickly to distant places and they don't belch grit and cinders.

Looking at the photograph, this isn't the message we get at all. There is a fair amount of window space, but nothing within light-years of the old station roof as far as visual interest goes. We see columns holding up some square roof sections, escalators, lines of budget-conscious railings and ticket counters. The floor is bland, with no texture or pattern to relieve the expanse, and was evidently designed more for the convenience of cleaning machines than the delight of visitors. We may also note the total absence of decoration of any kind, so that walls and ceilings, as well as the floor, are devoid of interest. It is an oddly disjointed collection of building parts and it exudes an air of sanitized brutality.

We can see this same space, with no effort of the imagination, as a factory for Hershey bars or Instant Breakfasts. Despite its size it is mean rather than grand, giving the impression of a place where crowds do not gather but are processed. While it undoubtedly cost a great deal of money, it looks cheap, uncared for and inelegant, and suggests constant use by faceless, indifferent, expendable pseudo-people.

It would not be difficult to assemble a book dealing

166 | How to See

only with big spaces, in which each was analyzed as a social mirror of a time and place. But here we are limited to a few arbitrarily selected illustrations, and a few notable contrasts. The intention is that once you get the idea, you can play these seeing games wherever you happen to be.

An entertaining aspect of the games is that the meanings are not always what one might expect them to be.

The Hall of Mirrors at Versailles is one of the stock "must see" items in the travel business. Built for Louis XIV, who is reputed to have been an egomaniac and a despot, it "makes a point of using noble materials such as marble, bronze, carved and gilded brass and copper," according to the French tourist bureau, and it has delighted visitors for generations. It is odd indeed that the tyrannical Sun King should have been responsible for such a space, while the output of modern democracy is mostly stage sets for Orwell's *1984*.

One of the very Orwellian interiors is in London's Heathrow Airport, another people-processing place filled with modernistic arrangements of lights and equipment and tired travelers.

The most cheerful of the new wave of *gallerias* is Philip Johnson's glittering Crystal Court in his

high-rise complex in Minneapolis. It is a thoroughly agreeable place to be, but it still cannot hold a candle to Milan's venerable Galleria. The moral, perhaps, is that even an architect as gifted as Johnson cannot break completely with the spirit of his own time.

One of the most beautiful of all modern big spaces is the Philharmonic Hall in West Berlin, designed by Hans Scharoun, which manages to combine a sense of intimacy with bigness by the use of multiple "trays" at different angles and levels. A marvelous place to listen to an orchestra. Scharoun designed it when he was a very old man, but one would never guess this from the youthful exuberance of his wonderful hollow sculpture.

Discontinuity

One of the things we never see in the urban landscape unless we deliberately go out and look for it is the remarkable number of patterns created by discontinuous elements. The forests of poles and wires, the skylines of TV antennas, the lighting in parking lots and along highways are all common examples. Even the movies shown in the jets on long trips are now presented on a kind of dotted line of miniscreens.

Since artists let very little go by them without some response in their work, it is not surprising to see a discontinuous column made of tubes and cables, by Kenneth Snelson; early (1941) paintings and drawings by Joan Miró; and the urban abstractions of Stuart Davis.

Visual Interruption

There is no reason why visual literacy should be higher among city officials than among others. Our towns are full of examples, funny or frustrating, of what happens when people put things in the urban landscape without looking at what they are doing.

The approach to a fine old windmill on Long Island is pockmarked by lighting standards and a rash of traffic signs. A very expensive sculpture by Henry Moore is placed so that there is nowhere from which it can be viewed with pleasure or comfort. A noble animal has to coexist with the local energy grid although they have little to do with each other. Benjamin Franklin is neatly split by some street lighting, and the monumental aluminum lady in Soviet Georgia has a similar problem. The prevailing inability to see is also reflected in the total absence of citizen complaints in the papers. But behind the defective vision lies something else as well: in bureaucracies nobody talks to anybody else.

Cities and Highways from the Air

One of the doors to seeing is a shift in the viewing platform, here accomplished by the airborne camera. Towns which look one way when seen from street level reveal a great deal about themselves when viewed from the air.

The art of reading such information has reached a degree of specialization hard for the layman to comprehend — a competent observer can apparently scan the records of a satellite passing over Mongolia and come up with information on the incidence of frostbite among the herdsmen.

Of the towns scanned by low-flying planes, one quickly notices a kind of family resemblance between Paris and Bath, and some connection with Popayán (page 178).

Saint Gall, on the other hand (page 179), is visibly indifferent to formal geometry, with a preference for meandering lines apparently generated by topography, for no other influence is in evidence.

Popayán is different from all the others in that its location is clearly tropical. The chimneys which pop out of the roofs of northern cities are absent here. The deep, dim courtyards belong in the siesta latitudes.

The big plaza, bare as a parade ground, is bordered by a large church (cathedral, probably). The other sides of the square are formed by three imposing buildings, none of them especially friendly in appearance.

One may guess that the civil and military powers are represented. At the very top of the picture, one has the impression of slums, right behind the imposing façade. The wealth, if this reading is correct, is

spread very thin. In consequence, one can hypothesize an intensive exploitation of the many poor by the few rich. This suggests a repressive, authoritarian government by the military, Church, or state, or some coalition.

It's not that difficult. Why don't you go and read Bath and Saint Gall?

But before you start, keep this in mind: Popayán is clearly an old city. The reading has to be based on what is seen. So it may be accurate for 1824, and not so good for 1976. It doesn't really matter, since the exercise is what matters. But generally speaking, it makes sense to check the date on the morning paper before quoting the editorial.

The story told by the highways is one of radical transformation: neither the countryside nor the urban environment will ever be quite the same again.

Man-Mades in the Natural Environment

A perennial source of pride for the race has been our ability to build big. Man, the helpless creature without fur, claws or supermuscles, finally realizes himself as a breed to be reckoned with by these demonstrations of intelligence and power. Apparently it has been that way from the beginning: from Stonehenge to the Seven Wonders of the World of the ancients, all these monuments have been greater than life size.

Today we are not quite as sure of the virtues of bigness, and there are social critics who now claim, with apparent justification, that "small is beautiful."

We can look at the illustrations and perhaps come to a slightly different conclusion. One is that modern technology has multiplied available energy enormously, but . . . one of the tiny handful of human artifacts that can be seen from the moon is the Great Wall of China.

Another observation we might make is that while bigness in itself does not look quite as glamorous as it did early in the century, there are clearly examples that seem to enhance the natural landscape in very dramatic and satisfying ways, such as river dams and hydraulic power installations. This is curious, for it gives us an insight into how we perceive beauty.

Beauty, when we strip away the aesthetic jargon, seems to mean fitness to purpose in the deepest and broadest sense. Nature, which has always been our model, never concerns itself with beauty, but always strives for total fitness to an environment. The thing I observe in the selected examples is that none of them pollutes air or water. Our grandparents rejoiced at the sight of smoke belching from factory chimneys because it meant jobs and prosperity. Today, for more and more of us, the sight is repellent, ugly, because we have begun to learn what the smoke does to the air we breathe. In this sense, our vision has changed with our broadened understanding and we see beauty in energy produced without pollution. Beauty, in other words, really does lie in the beholder.

Transparencies

The universal delight in transparency goes back to very small children peeking through their fingers, and in architecture, to huge, small-paned windows built before 1600. Part of the appeal of scuba diving is that it takes one through the looking glass into unsuspected water worlds of fantastic richness.

Transparent building took its great leap in the mid-1800s, when metal structures came into wide use, and factories learned to make glass in large sheets. Architects, engineers and the public responded to the new possibilities with enormous enthusiasm, and we have yet to match structures like Sir Joseph Paxton's Crystal Palace of 1851 (page 186), the vaulted Galleria of Milan (page 165) and the great railroad sheds of London and New York's Pennsylvania Station (page 166), lost a few years back to "progress."

Fashions in transparency change like everything else. Our own contributions include mirrored buildings (transparent only at night, when the inside lights are on), see-through blouses, glass elevators and plastic roofs. Technically some of these new things are interesting, but few of them show the curlicued exuberance of the earlier examples.

As a matter of fact, as our exercises in seeing go on, it is hard to find any building in the contemporary scene that could be fairly described as "exuberant." Too much of what we see has been designed by computers which tell the boys in the drafting room what to draw.

Survival Designs

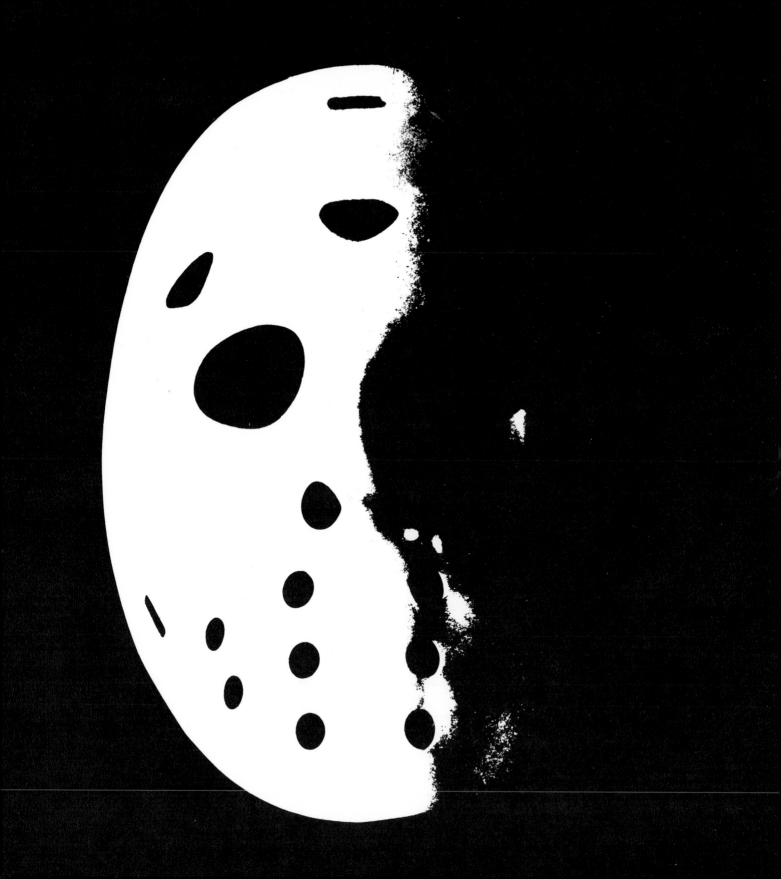

Survival Design

Living in the urban world, as most of us do, our seeing is more likely to focus on man-made objects than on nature. We are more likely to see a passenger plane in the air than a flock of geese. The meandering stream is a rarity, and trees are pegged into sidewalks much like lampposts.

The first thing we have to cope with, in looking at the synthetic environment, is that everything in it has been designed. Manhole covers and mailboxes do not just happen: someone has to figure out how they should be made, exactly what they are supposed to do, and how they might look. This has to happen every time something new is plugged into the city network, whether it's a hundred-story building or a fire hydrant. Then someone has to make accurate drawings and specifications so that the item can be manufactured or built.

As one might expect, there are good designs and bad designs. One of the reasons for the repellent aspect of most parts of most cities is that no one has thought about them as overall designs, so we get a helter-skelter effect as a result of plugging in buildings and services on a snap-decision basis, without any concern for their surroundings.

People who buy things make decisions on the basis of whether they like the design or not, since they rarely have any way of knowing how well the product will work after they get it home. The trouble with such design decisions is that visual illiterates have no way of knowing whether a design is any good or not. This is why the interiors of most houses look as if they had been put together by the blind. Most motel rooms are equally tasteless and mediocre, probably because the management wants its customers to relax in a familiar, "homelike" environment.

This is not a book about design, but since there is so much of it around, we cannot ignore its existence entirely.

Design is a process: one starts with a need, a problem, and ends up with a design for a thing. The basic rules are not complicated: a designed object has to do what it was made for. We use flowers for

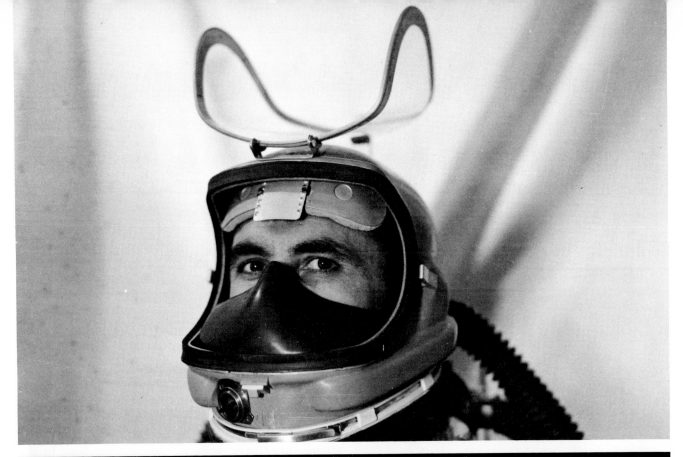

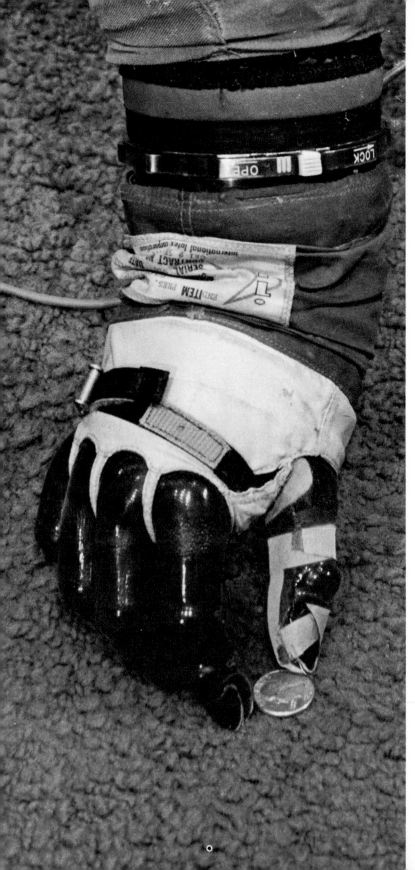

decoration, but a flowering plant is a very busy organism. It has to collect solar energy, and take in nourishment through its root system. It has to attract insects for pollination, and it has to manufacture seeds after the bloom has served its purpose. If we look at a flower carefully and study its details, we come to realize that it looks exactly like what it does.

There is no better description of a successful man-made design. A pen looks as if it can write, a kite looks as if it can fly. A thing that does not look like what it does, such as a color television set in a cabinet that tries to look like a relic from a château on the Loire, is a bad joke and it merely reveals the illiteracy of the owner and the cupidity of the manufacturer.

To make a very, very good design, not merely an adequate one, is an exceedingly difficult job, and the job gets harder as the result moves toward perfection. Difficulty means high energy expenditure which in turn means time and money. It was not surprising to read that the little vehicle shot to the moon cost $17,000,000, although we are very good at manufacturing vehicles that sell for less. In the industrial process, first-class designs such as bicycles can be sold reasonably, partly because the design process has been going on for generations, and also because the tooling costs can be amortized over thousands or millions of units.

The best designs we know about (outside of nature, where all organisms fit into this category) are survival designs. A plane is a survival design: it either flies properly or it will presently kill its crew and passengers. Space and deep-sea equipment are survival designs; and so is most military hardware. Survival designs are the best for the simple reason that the user's life is riding on their performance. Armor is obsolete survival design, but we do not think less of it because it cannot stop a bullet. Much sporting equipment, which includes some of the best of all modern designs, can be classed as survival design, not only because the danger of serious injury is real, but because most sports are a symbolic acting out of battles or duels.

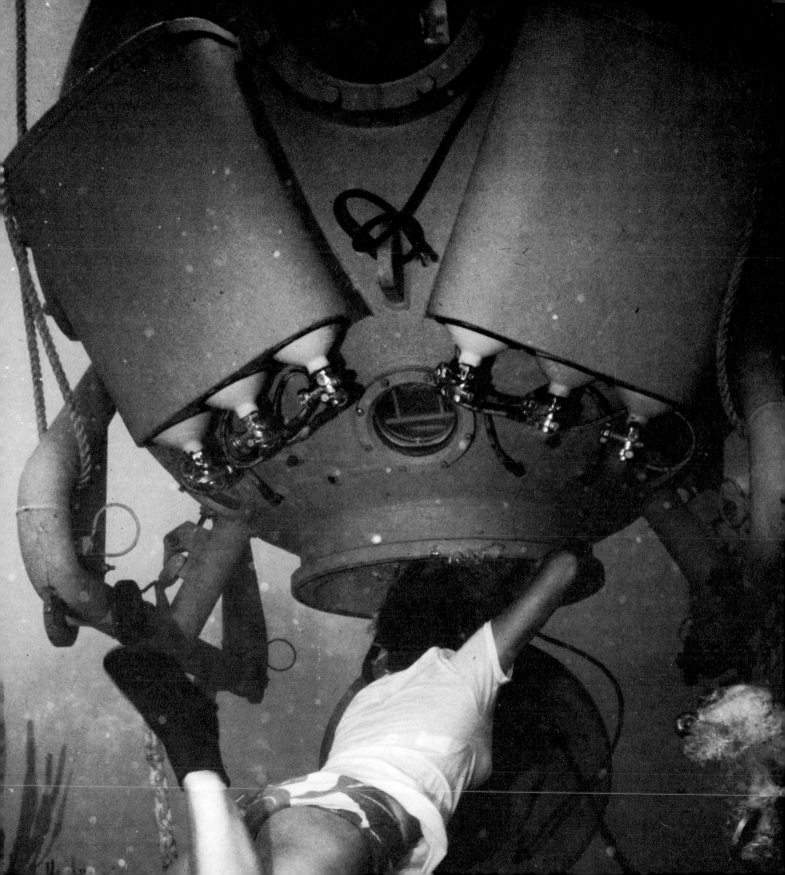

Armor

Style is the visible expression of what a thing is and does. A snake has a serpentine style. Armor is designed to keep its wearer alive. It has to be tough, as light as possible, flexible enough to allow its user to get on a horse or to fight on foot.

Armor follows two main lines in all designs: it uses metal plates, hinged or pivoted, or it uses chain mail. The mesh is lighter and more flexible, the metal plates are more resistant to thrusts and blows. Some armor uses a combination of the two methods.

Japanese armor, sometimes made of hard leather fastened with thongs and cords, looks very different from medieval Western examples, but there is not that much difference between them in concept. After all, they had the same job to do.

An interesting tidbit we get from the illustrations is that preindustrial craftsmen rarely stopped at bare functional expression. The two helmets were clearly designed to identify as well as protect their owners; the footpiece is richly decorated; the Japanese corselet, possibly more for ceremonial use than combat, is a marvel of elegant workmanship.

What all survival designs have in common, whether plain or decorated, is a look of absolute *rightness*. This is why we find obsolete fighting equipment in art museums.

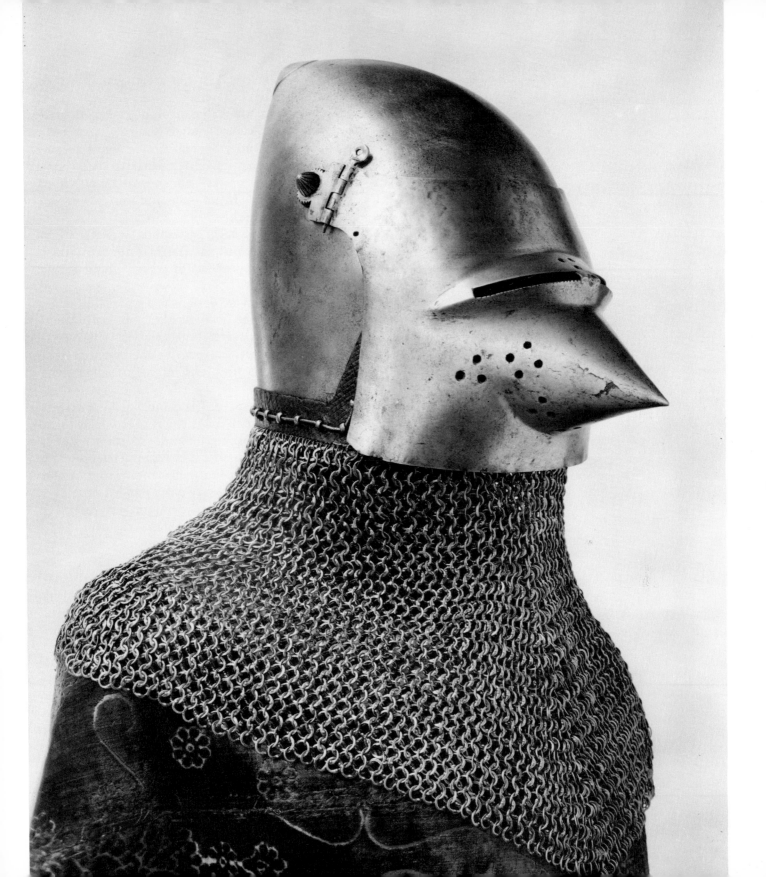

Sport

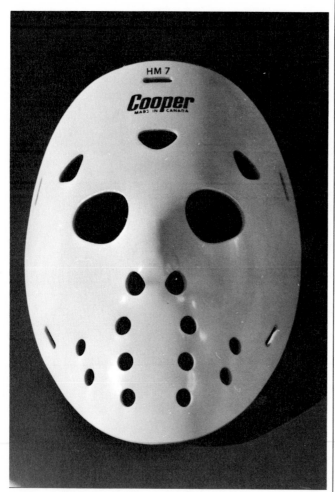

If sporting goods were sold in art museums, would we perceive them differently?

Modern populations, the involuntary beneficiaries and victims of science and technology, are rarely able to see anything, beyond simple identification. Design, for the average individual, is decoration applied to a cake or car, a marzipan flower or an "opera" window. In consequence the stores are crammed with kitsch.

To break out of such patterns it is necessary to accept the proposition that design is not decoration, but an integral expression of what a thing is and does.

The best man-made designs are survival designs, simply because they deal with life and death rather than marketing considerations. How does the relatively commonplace, inexpensive equipment used in competitive sports find itself in such exalted company?

Consider, for instance, the simple mask at left. It is a one-piece, factory-made object of molded plastic. Even if we know nothing about the sport for which it is intended, we know that it is a commercial product (the maker's name is on it). It is meant to protect a face (we see the eyeholes and the molded nose cavity), and it does this with the minimum weight and material, which in turn suggests that the user has to move quickly. Whether the danger comes from sticks or flying balls, the eyeholes tell us the minimum size of such objects, for anything smaller might get through. We feel safe in assuming that the smaller holes are for ventilation, and possibly weight reduction. Four slits at the edges accept straps for holding the mask to the head. The visual clues are clear, but we are left with a mystery. Why does this simple commercial product take on the monumental, timeless aspect of the oldest sculptural creations? I believe that we have more than a visual trick here: the irreducible perfection of the object is enough to put it into the mainstream of great design.

Games have symbolic meanings, some related to life-and-death confrontations, seen in the competitive nature of sports. Competition identifies strengths and isolates weaknesses. In sports, the chances of winning are influenced by the design of the equipment, a fact which leads to intense concentration on minute details. Back around the turn of the century, many American millionaires became engrossed in sulky racing and things reached the point where one owner offered his carriage maker a thousand dollars for each ounce he could take out without loss of strength. An ounce is not much, and a thousand dollars was a very substantial sum in those days.

In baseball there are three basic categories of equipment: the ball, the bat and the glove. The first two are shared by players on both teams; the third is personal, used by only a single player. One might think that one perfect glove could meet all needs, but there are at least three clearly defined types, each closely matched to the role of the player.

Furthermore, an examination of each glove shows something that has almost disappeared from consumer products: a visible concern for quality of materials and workmanship that extends to every detail. It is strange: the evidence of loving care we associate with the best preindustrial craftsmen suddenly surfaces again in articles produced for a highly commercialized mass sport.

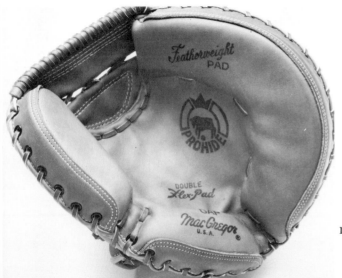

Wherever we look the story repeats itself. The design tells us in each instance what the object is and does, and always in terms of doing the most with the least. One might think that this constant drive to achieve high performance with an absolute economy of means would lead to monotonous standardization, but instead we encounter endless delicate variations.

The racing bike looks at first glance like any other bicycle, but we presently notice that there are no

gears, no brakes, none of the conveniences. The problem was to design a bicycle that would go fastest with the least effort for the rider. Thus we come to a design that is the essence of the concept "bicycle."

Sports equipment, viewed as design, moves into the top rank of man-made products because of the extreme efforts put into it by people who are in the rare position of craftsmen-designers, asked only to meet the highest performance levels in whatever way they think best.

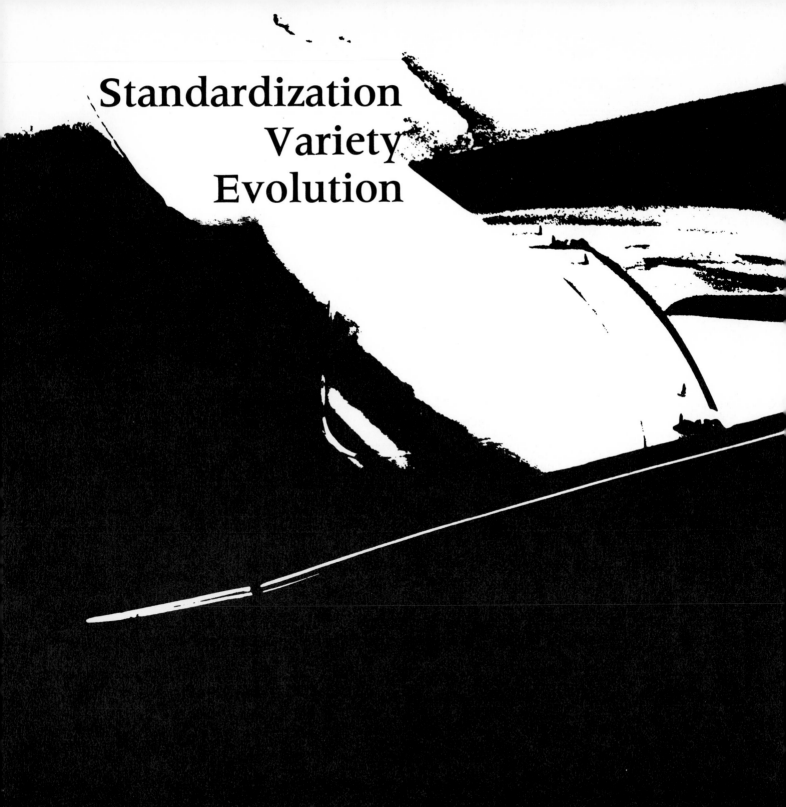

Standardization
Variety
Evolution

Standardization

The man-made environment is full of things that are all alike: mailboxes, hot dogs, cops-and-robbers shows, Republicans and Democrats, lead pencils, topless office buildings, political speeches, traffic lights.

We call this standardization, and it has become a favorite whipping boy. The variety that adds spice to life, we feel, evaporates when everything gets to be as alike as two peas, forgetting that one of the things we like about peas is that they are alike. It would really be no improvement at all, in our view, if every fifth pea were the size of a golf ball. Anyway, peas have to be alike to fit into the pods that protect them until they mature.

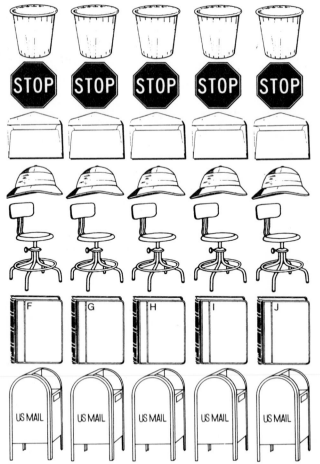

If we are going to blame the ills of a mass industrial society on standardization, we have the villain. The subject is an interesting one, however, and it could stand some probing. The first question is, what do we mean? There is standardization among organisms, but in nature we encounter the miracle of unity encompassing infinite diversity. No two peas are exactly alike; if two ball bearings are not identical they do not perform properly. We might play with the idea that organic and inorganic standardization are different. All 35-mm films fit all 35-mm cameras. All stop signs in the United States are octagonal. All wallets fit pockets. All cars have just about the same driving controls in the same positions. All pay phones accept nickels, dimes and quarters. What a mess our lives would be if this were not the case!

A plant manager deals with an output of standard products and an input of standard people. But what a difference in the "standard"! The products (he hopes) are identical; the people are intelligent, stupid, lazy, energetic, healthy, ill, generous, selfish, kind, vicious, loyal, hostile. It is no wonder that industry automates and computerizes wherever it can, although this is by no means the only reason it does so.

The problems arise, not from the fact of standardization, but when the organic and inorganic

varieties get confused with each other. Then we begin to hear from the social psychologists about the evils of a technological society's efforts to "thingify" people. These evils are real enough, heaven knows, and they reach their peak in the police states which have become so prominent a political feature of the twentieth century.

Let us go on with the question of how standardized organisms respond to standardized things. We can agree, I think, that there are all sorts of items we accept in which uniformity appears to us to be a virtue. But not all items. We could construct a kind of spectrum, with acceptance and rejection at opposite ends. Disposables, such as gas lighters, razors and toothpicks, seem to create no resistance at all. Goods held in common, such as mailboxes and manhole covers, are in the same category, assuming that anyone even looks at them. Sameness in gas stations of a given brand, or in chain eating places, is viewed as a convenience.

When we get to cars, the climate changes. While for many the car has become an essential service and nothing more, there are others for whom the car is a mark of status or individuality. Here the evidence of concern is found in the model or brand and it extends all the way to customizing (VW Beetle with Rolls radiator) to decorative repainting. Still, no one objects to the evident economies in mass production.

The case of the tract house is similar to that of the car, but the desire to "personalize" the uniform product is stronger. The individual color scheme, add-ons that create "diamond pane" windows, a perfect patch of lawn, plastic squirrels on the roofs are some of the familiar devices employed.

Oddly enough, these efforts to establish an individual identity are also severely restricted in the lower middle class housing tracts. It is okay to be different, but not really different. There are cases where an irate neighborhood has taken legal action against a deviant: a modern flattop in a "Colonial"

development. There are also cases of arson to get rid of an offending design.

As the object involved — a car or home — becomes more closely intertwined with personal identity or status, feelings can run very high. It is not so much a rejection of uniformity as a complex interplay of desires for identity mixed with insecurity — feelings so strong that a genuine expression of individuality is seen as a threat. This, basically, is one of the main reasons that housing tracts are so bad; no designer can deal with such a mix of contradictions, especially for groups way up on the scale of visual literacy. The tracts are mirror images of the people who live in them.

When these tracts are extended to the dimensions reached in the giant cities, they become interminable, loathsome nightmares, and by their physical aspect alone make the most violent criticisms of modern society seem like understatement. Any examination of the various meanings of standardization takes us to the question of numbers.

Let me present an absurd example to make the point. The Parthenon, in Athens, is considered to have been one of the great buildings of antiquity, and its golden ruins are now a perennial darling of the travel agents. It had a surround of forty-six Doric columns, each seemingly identical to all the others. Wrapped in a rectangular bundle under a gable roof, they must have looked very fine indeed. The Greeks of that time were probably the best stonecutters on earth. Part of the pull of this building on the imagination was its location on the Acropolis, a superb urban site if there ever was one.

Now we have to imagine a developer, so pleased with this building that he builds an exact replica next to it. And another, and another, until the Acropolis is crammed to bursting with Parthenons. Somehow the idea of a trip to Greece becomes less appealing . . .

Absurd as this image may be, it becomes tragic in the example of the housing tract. Accepting the fact that the quality of the original model is inferior to begin with, the multiplication to 1,000 units, to 10,000 units, is more than the mind, eye or spirit can support. The scale is no longer human.

Yet there are plenty of villages in existence to make the point that uniform house design on a small scale can produce extremely pleasant environments.

Perfect Design

Our title is open to challenge: it is reasonable enough to assert that nothing is perfect; if this were not so, things would never change. But for our limited purposes here, a perfect design is one so good that no one, over generations or centuries, has been able to make a basic improvement. The umbrella, or parasol, is a case in point.

The umbrella has been around since ancient times and was rediscovered in Europe in the sixteenth century. When the Japanese version emerged I have no idea. Both, as far as concept goes, are identical: a sheet of paper or fabric, loosely fastened to flexible ribs, hangs around a stick. A sliding ring on the stick, connected to a second set of ribs, can be pushed to the point where the tension in the fabric and the resistance of the ribs come into a kind of dynamic balance. The loose fabric then becomes taut as a drumhead, providing a surface for the rain to bounce off.

While improved gadgetry has been introduced, the umbrella remains fundamentally unchanged. Perfect or not, it is a marvelous design: lightweight, portable, impermeable, beautiful.

The track bike tells the same story: faster and lighter than its predecessors, it is still an affair with two lightweight wheels, a frame, seat, handlebars and pedals. You can speed up the bike by adding a motor, but then it isn't a bicycle anymore, but something else, with its own qualities and a whole new set of design problems.

Scissors, in the West, are invariably two crossing cutting edges, finger grips, and a pivot in between. The designs vary all over the lot, from heavy, crudely forged and filed, to scissors of extreme delicacy. Whatever the size or use, the concept of the tool never varies.

The old wooden barrel, built of shaped spokes held together by bands of steel, is also under attack: both aluminum and plastics have provided competitive products. Even with the change of material, however, the barrel shape, designed for easy rolling, has yet to be improved upon, while the wine industry continues to find wood an ideal aging material.

The barrel, viewed as a structure, is not that far from the umbrella. The barrel itself, made of shaped wood staves, has a tendency to give way when filled with liquid; the metal rings resist this pressure and hold the barrel together. Within limits, the greater the internal pressure, the tighter the barrel.

The same look of inevitability characterizes the incandescent light bulb. The first lamp filaments burned in a vacuum, and the domed shape is ideal for resisting the pressure of the normal, sea-level atmosphere. The nipple on top of the antique pear-shaped bulb was the orifice through which the air was pumped out; later, the little tube was softened by heat and sealed. Modern bulbs contain an inert gas, as a rule, and are shaped to resist crushing and to leave room enough inside for the filament to glow in an oxygen-free atmosphere. As the photograph suggests, the oldest and newest incandescent bulbs are not much different from each other: filament, bulb, and socket are clearly to be seen, regardless of age.

One of the oddest of these perfect designs, odd because it is so utterly commonplace, is the lead pencil. Despite such inventions as the mechanical pencil, ball-point and felt pen, lead pencils are still made and sold in large quantities. Among the virtues of the lead pencil are the flat sides, which discourage rolling off the desk, the built-in eraser, and the fact that the pencil, normally encased in cedar, smells good when being sharpened.

Design:
Articulated
to Closed

We are accustomed to think of evolution as a process limited to the natural world. Eohippus, after millennia of mutation and selection, became the horse. Suns get old and become novas. Dinosaurs and the creaking pterodactyl are no more.

The same process, enormously accelerated, goes on in the man-made world through design. The evolutionary changes are sometimes so rapid that we perceive them as shifts in fashion. But even here, looking at four products that have spread all over the world, the evolution from invention to present-day form took place in not more than a hundred years, a split second in the life of the planet.

Design evolution in artifacts goes on much as it does in nature: a series of shifting adaptations to environment and a variety of pressures, and much like the biologists, we can study the changes in form and "read" them to learn what produced them. These forces vary greatly in power and magnitude; generally speaking they are social, technical and economic — in other words, they represent the entire social environment, physical laws, plus an infusion of human irrationality.

To take an inconsequential example, the earliest cars often came with whip holders. This was partly because carriages came with these accessories (the first car designers had no other model before them), and partly because horses were sometimes needed when the cars broke down. In a short time both reasons for them disappeared and so did the whip holders.

One curious aspect of evolution in design is that it seems to go along the same lines: the basic similarities between cars, planes, trains and typewriters are hard to find, for they do very different things and they come in an extreme range of sizes. But in every instance, we note a highly articulated design at the beginning, and then a steady movement in the direction of an entirely closed form.

In case the terms are unfamiliar in this context, "articulated" means that the working parts are out in the open and can be seen and understood. It is the difference between a grasshopper and a porpoise, an old pendulum clock and a digital watch.

If we could run through a time-lapse film of the car since 1900, we would actually see all kinds of exposed parts vanish, one by one, inside the body: fenders, running boards, headlights, gas tanks, hand brakes, horns, spare tires and others. Even the windshield wipers have disappeared from today's cars, except when in use.

The famous Chrysler Airflow was a failure in the marketplace because it moved up the evolutionary scale too fast. The public, like nature, is extremely conservative and resists change when it moves beyond an acceptable pace.

We can understand the evolution from articulated to closed more easily in some cases than in others. It is now obvious to us that the modern plane becomes safer and more efficient as it goes faster. (The Wright brothers' plane, if towed by a jet, would disintegrate.) The process is harder to understand in the case of an object, say a sewing machine, which rarely goes anywhere.

One answer lies in the manufacturing process: the working parts of the early sewing machines were hand-shaped on lathes and other machine tools. As metal stamping, plastic forming, injection molding and production lines came in, and as subassemblies were installed to save money, time, space and weight, the insides of machines became less interesting and also less comprehensible. Open a pocket calculator and what do you see? A few printed circuits and a battery. So it made sense to close things in.

Another reason lies in the goals of technology, which include a drive to do more and more with less and less. Thus reduced bulk and weight — miniaturization — becomes a symbol for success. The plane is one of the most prestigious of all such symbols, which means that we accept the look of a plane as the proper modern look. It was not coincidence that as the streamlining appropriate at propeller speeds evolved into the sharp edges of the jets, car styling went through a matching change. The logic that operated in the case of planes had little to do with cars. They just "looked" better.

Now something else is brewing: lunar modules and the satellites are not closed designs at all. They bristle with bumps, vanes, antennas and other exposed hardware, none of which creates problems of movement in a hard vacuum. The articulation is by no means complete, of course, for their insides are crammed full of miniaturized equipment. But, since satellites are even more prestigious than planes, in a technical sense, what effects will their new look have on earthside products?

No one knows yet, but what a fine opportunity to use our eyes to figure out what might happen next!

Typewriters

It would take a specialist engineer to fully appreciate the subtleties of evolution in typewriter design, but there is no difficulty in observing the transformation. Incidentally, there is also an example of "reverse evolution" in the disappearance of the earlier typing cylinders in favor of separate keys and their later "rediscovery" by IBM and Olivetti.

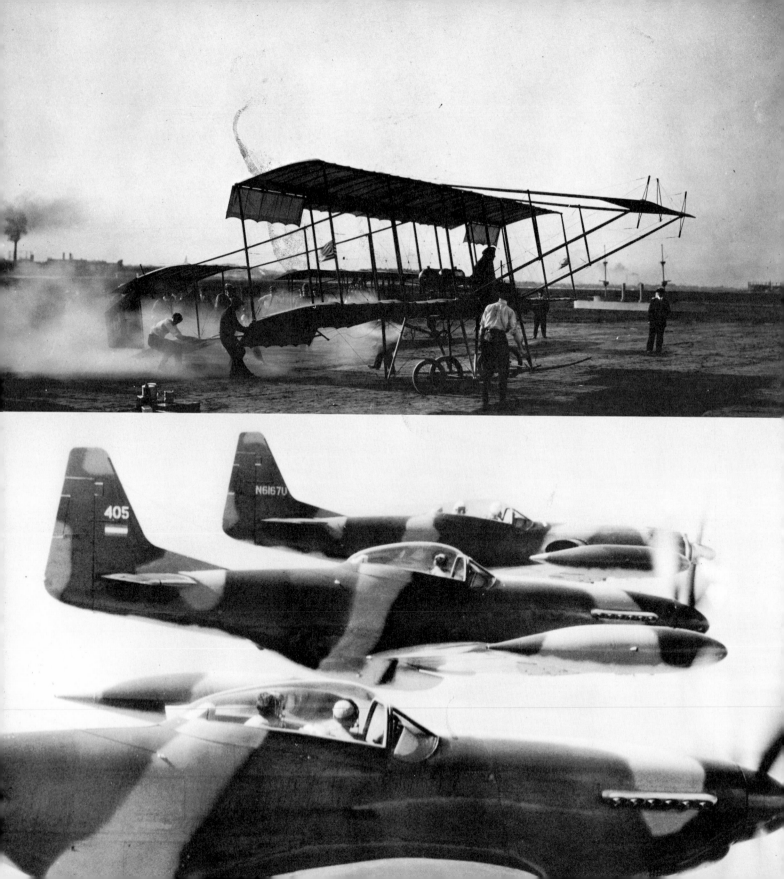

Air-Space Vehicles

The photographs show clearly what has happened in aircraft design. The unmanned Viking, a sample of the "new" look, is of course not an aircraft at all, but there is nothing wrong with the speed at which it flies.

Trains

Mass transit has come in for a new look as a response to air poisoned by car exhausts and to the escalating costs of energy.

Japan's Tokkaido Express is the fastest "conventional" train, averaging about 125 mph on its automated runs between Tokyo and Osaka. At 150 mph or thereabouts, wheels become unreliable, and most experimental designs now depend on air support or magnetic repulsion to replace wheels. The great pioneer in this field is Jean Bertin's Aérotrain, which used turbo props for propulsion, then rocket motors (207 mph in 1967), and has since turned to linear induction motors. The interesting thing about these is that they are invisible, nonpolluting and noiseless.

The Automobile

Here we have the articulated-to-closed story in one of its most striking forms. During the early years, everything is hung on the outside; then everything gradually vanishes within the shell. We have here only a 1906 design as a reminder, a pair of tail fins as a symbol of passing fashion at its most lethal, and a more recent example to bring us up to date. For any car buff who feels shortchanged, a good book on classic cars will fill the gaps.

Something else to keep in mind: the U.S. passenger car is, among other things, a status item with strong overtones of fashion styling. Hence it takes many of its ideas from planes, which are not fashion items.

The Four Hundred Faces

Just how much any of us sees of the most intimate personal environments is an open question. Can you describe the colors and pattern of any rug in your dwelling? The wallpaper in the bedroom? The pictures in the front hall? When were they last looked at?

Right here it occurred to me that I might try this game myself and I scored very badly. In the course of trying to see our living room with a fresh eye, I noticed some faces, and was presently involved in an inventory: faces in one living room. A face, by my scoring system, was human or animal, printed or painted or carved or photographed. As it turned out there were some four-hundred-plus faces, visible and waiting to be counted, in that one room. I would have guessed a dozen. They are there, but they just don't jump out at you.

After the inventory had been checked and put away, out came the camera, and a rainy, boring Sunday afternoon was transformed by hours of arranging and lighting and exposing. Seeing things is an intellectual-aesthetic exercise which increases one's inalienable capital: riches that can be accumulated without cost and, once acquired, cannot be lost or stolen. It was Thomas Jefferson who said something of the sort about intellectual pleasures; I am sure he would be the last to object to the addition of visual, or even audiovisual, delights.

Kokeshi

The *kokeshi* is a traditional doll of Japan, whose origins go back to remote antiquity. It is made of hard maple, and consists of a ball-shaped head on a cylindrical body. The amazing thing is the number of variations on this simple theme.

Because the making of these lovely dolls is an ancient craft, it is not surprising that the various designs "belong" to individual artists, or families, and are handed down from father to son. For this reason, the dolls are always signed. No artist would dream of copying another's design, and while an occasional modern expression is to be found, the craft, like all such activities everywhere, is dying out.

For the children, the remarkable property of these dolls is that their total simplicity encourages the use of imagination, including the instant transformation from plaything to weapon when the kids get mad at each other.

Buttons

A push button is a device, unbeatable in its elegant simplicity, that opens or closes an electric circuit. It can set into motion machines of immense power, activate a lighter, or send off an ICBM.

The button is utterly neutral, does nothing but wait for the approach of a finger, and, because of the disparity between the light touch and possibly massive consequences, it has become a metaphor for modern power fantasies. Any idiot can push it. It is the communion wafer of technocratic society.

Small wonder, then, that consumer products have a lot of buttons on them. The greater the number of buttons, the more potent the user becomes, and the deeper the relief from feelings of insecurity.

There may be reasons for the prodigious increase in the button population, but logic alone does not explain the fifteen buttons on a blender, since one rotary switch could do the same job. The unchallenged top product of our time is the pocket calculator, reported to have racked up sales of twenty million units. Ostensibly this is because it can add and multiply faster than its owner, but I suspect the real reason is that it is the first small product that consists of practically nothing but buttons.

Bread

Bread — the staff of life, sacred, the beginning of civilization, the bond: people who break bread together are different from others; they may not fight, or betray each other.

The levels of meaning in bread are bottomless. At surface level, it is bought in a certain quantity, for a price, to last so many days. One level down: breads have shapes and sizes, different kinds of flour, different textures. Some make better toast. Down again: breads are symbolic, religious, sexual, tied to places and times. Matzo is for Passover, not the Fourth of July.

Bread is made from dough, which is a plastic substance, like clay. It can be twisted, stretched, coiled, pushed into molds; parts can be modeled separately and then put together before baking. It can be pricked, streaked, engraved. It can be baked so that some parts get darker than others. Bread is a celebration: it goes with wine, lovers and life.

It is also a mass consumer item, produced in standard trays, controlled ovens, and untouched by any baker's hands. It is now designed like a brick, modular, so that it will fit baking pans, conveyors, delivery vans, standard supermarket shelves. It comes wrapped in packages by graphic designers, sealed for freshness, sliced for the convenience of tired mothers, enriched with the vitamins removed in bleaching the flour.

So the long and glorious history of bread ends with it as the perfect textureless standardized loaf, predictable, fabricated with trustworthy synthetics, the dream food for the nonpeople.

I hear that quite a few people are learning to bake, again.

Designed by Mitchell Ford
Typeset in Herman Zapf's Aldus by DEKR Corporation
Printed and bound by Murray Printing Company
Text stock: Patina, from the S. D. Warren Company
Bound in Fictionette, from Columbia Mills